W9-CGM-361

Discovering the World of Geography

Grades 7–8

By
MYRL SHIREMAN

COPYRIGHT © 2003 Mark Twain Media, Inc.

ISBN   10-digit: 1-58037-230-9
        13-digit: 978-1-58037-230-5

Printing No. CD-1576

Mark Twain Media, Inc., Publishers
Distributed by Carson-Dellosa Publishing LLC

Visit us at www.carsondellosa.com

Table of Contents

Introduction

The 18 National Geography Standards have been developed to ensure that students in the United States are competitive on an international basis. To become competitive internationally, it is necessary that students first have the basic geographic knowledge that is required to think analytically.

This book for grades seven or eight has been written as the capstone for a series of four books for grades four through eight. Each book has been written with many activities devoted to developing the basic understandings students must have to meet the standards. Other activities are then developed to address individual standards.

In this book, chapters devoted to developing the basic skills foundation are followed with a pretest activity and a final test. The pretests are designed in a completion format so students can be successful. The final tests are a multiple-choice format based on the pretest. Other chapters do not have a pretest and final test format because the activities in the chapter are designed to help students develop deeper insights and become more analytical as they study the Eastern Hemisphere.

Teachers are encouraged to make transparencies from the book. Because the knowledge level varies from class to class, student success on selected activities may be significantly improved if completed under teacher direction.

National Geography Standards

Teachers leading discussions while completing units and activities is a prerequisite for accomplishing the standards. Inquiry discussion is important: *What do you know? How are things alike and not alike? Why do you think that?*

National Standard 1: *How to use maps and other geographic representations, tools, and technologies to acquire, process, and report information*

This standard is addressed through map, chart, and graph activities in a number of chapters. Units 1, 4, 6, and 7 especially utilize maps and other representations. This standard is also addressed in the Unit 13 Problems.

National Standard 4: *The physical and human characteristics of place*

This standard is addressed in activities throughout the book. Units 1–9 explore the physical and human characteristics of the Eastern Hemisphere. Unit 10 and Unit 11 focus on the characteristics of place that make a specific area a "hot spot" of conflict or strategic importance.

National Standard 9: *The characteristics, distributions, and migrations of human populations on Earth's surface*

Activities in Unit 2 address this standard as students learn about the populations of Eastern Hemisphere nations. Unit 8 also addresses population density. The standard is also addressed in the Unit 13 Problems.

National Standard 11: *The patterns and networks of economic interdependence on Earth's surface*

This standard is addressed in Unit 11 as students learn of the importance of Eastern Hemisphere nations to the rest of the world for their resources and locations.

National Standard 12: *The process, patterns, and functions of human settlement*

Throughout the book, students address this standard as they learn how physical features, natural resources, agriculture, and climate affect human settlement. The standard is specifically addressed in Unit 3 and Unit 5.

National Standard 13: *Understanding cooperation and conflict*

This standard is specifically addressed in Unit 10, which focuses on conflicts within countries and between countries.

National Standard 14: *How human actions modify the environment*

This standard is addressed in Unit 12 and in the Unit 13 Problems as students learn about the human factors in desertification, salinization, and flooding.

National Standard 15: *How physical systems affect human systems*

This standard is addressed in Units 3, 4, 5, and 7 as students learn how physical features affect the climate and the desirability of a region for settlement, transportation, commerce, and agriculture.

National Standard 17: *How to apply geography to interpret the past*

Students address this standard in Unit 3 and Unit 5 as they learn how geography has affected the development of cities in various countries.

Name: _____   Date: _____

Unit 1: Political Geography of the Eastern Hemisphere

A. Continents

Use **Map 1** and **an atlas** to complete the following. Place the number on the blank that locates the continent.

1. Asia   2. Europe   3. Africa   4. Australia   5.   Antarctica

MAP 1

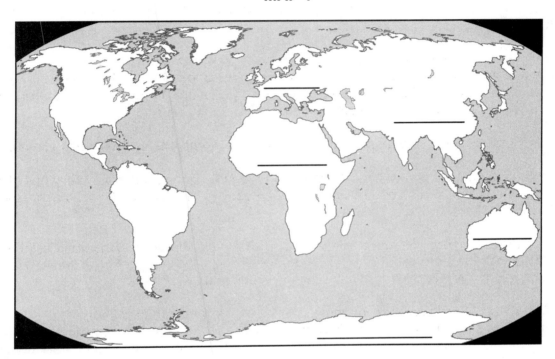

B. Countries

Use **Map 2** and **an atlas** to complete the following. A blank is located inside or near the boundary of each country listed below. Place the letter on the blank that correctly locates the country. Write the abbreviation for the continent on which the country is located on the blank below, next to each country. **AS = Asia, E = Europe, AF = Africa, AU = Australia**.

a. Russia _____   b. Algeria _____   c. France _____

d. India _____   e. Sweden _____   f. Ukraine _____

g. Egypt _____   h. Iran _____   i. Saudi Arabia _____

j. Nigeria _____   k. Indonesia _____   l. Japan _____

m. Philippines _____   n. Sudan _____   o. Libya _____

p. South Africa _____   q. Angola _____   r. Kenya _____

s. Tanzania _____   t. Mozambique _____   u. Democratic Republic of Congo _____

v. Thailand _____   w. Myanmar _____   x. Pakistan _____

y. Vietnam _____   z. Turkey _____   aa. Mali _____   bb. Zimbabwe _____

Name: _____   Date: _____

Unit 1: Political Geography of the Eastern Hemisphere

B. Countries (cont.)

MAP 2

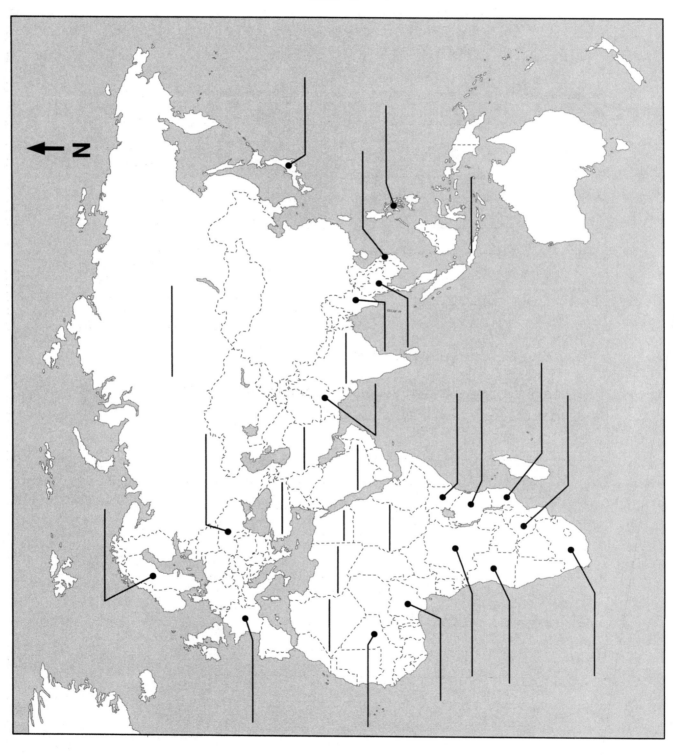

Name: _____   Date: _____

Unit 1: Political Geography of the Eastern Hemisphere

B. Countries (cont.)

Use **Map 3** to complete the following. On Map 3, a blank is located near the boundary of the countries listed below. Place the letter that identifies the country on the blank on Map 3 to correctly locate each country. Complete each of the blanks below by writing the name of the continent on which the country is located.

a. Afghanistan _____   b. Tajikistan _____

c. Austria _____   d. Switzerland _____

e. Mali _____   f. Botswana _____

g. Jordan _____   h. Uzbekistan _____

i. Mongolia _____   j. Hungary _____

k. Czech Republic _____   l. Slovakia _____

m. Armenia _____   n. Chad _____

o. Niger _____   p. Zambia _____

q. Zimbabwe _____

Use **Map 2** and **Map 3** to complete the following.

1. The location of a country is very important. Compare the countries on Map 2 and Map 3. How does the location of the countries on Map 2 differ from the countries on Map 3? Write your findings on the blanks below.

   _____

   _____

   _____

   _____

2. What is an important location advantage the countries on Map 2 have that the countries on Map 3 do not have?

   _____

   _____

   _____

   _____

Name: _____ Date: _____

Unit 1: Political Geography of the Eastern Hemisphere

B. Countries (cont.)

MAP 3

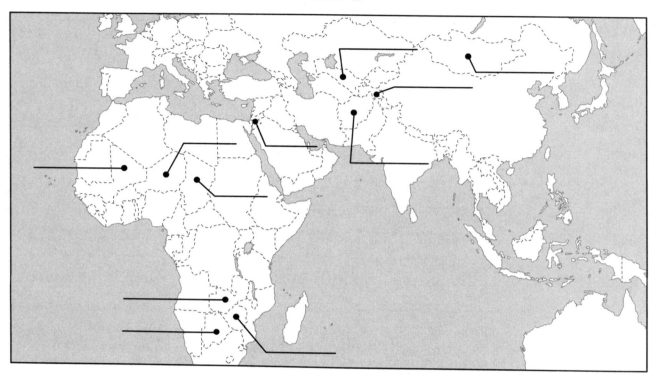

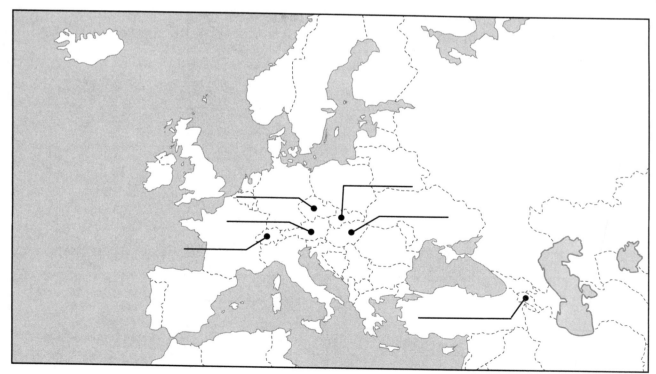

Name: _____ Date: _____

Unit 1: Political Geography of the Eastern Hemisphere

C. Pretest Practice

Place a plus sign (+) on the blank to show the continent of which each country is a part. If a country is a part of two continents, place a plus (+) on the blank for each continent.

Country	Asia	Africa	Australia	Europe
1. India	_____	_____	_____	_____
2. Nigeria	_____	_____	_____	_____
3. Libya	_____	_____	_____	_____
4. France	_____	_____	_____	_____
5. Kenya	_____	_____	_____	_____
6. Iran	_____	_____	_____	_____
7. Thailand	_____	_____	_____	_____
8. Sweden	_____	_____	_____	_____
9. Indonesia	_____	_____	_____	_____
10. Ukraine	_____	_____	_____	_____
11. Turkey	_____	_____	_____	_____
12. Saudi Arabia	_____	_____	_____	_____
13. Vietnam	_____	_____	_____	_____
14. Myanmar	_____	_____	_____	_____
15. Dem. Rep. of the Congo	_____	_____	_____	_____
16. Afghanistan	_____	_____	_____	_____
17. Iraq	_____	_____	_____	_____
18. Finland	_____	_____	_____	_____
19. Denmark	_____	_____	_____	_____
20. Jordan	_____	_____	_____	_____
21. Israel	_____	_____	_____	_____
22. Switzerland	_____	_____	_____	_____
23. South Africa	_____	_____	_____	_____
24. Australia	_____	_____	_____	_____
25. Philippines	_____	_____	_____	_____
26. Russia	_____	_____	_____	_____
27. Chad	_____	_____	_____	_____
28. Egypt	_____	_____	_____	_____
29. Spain	_____	_____	_____	_____
30. Czech Republic	_____	_____	_____	_____

Name: _____ Date: _____

Unit 1: Political Geography of the Eastern Hemisphere

C. Test

Complete each blank using the continent names: **Africa, Asia, Europe, Australia**.

Country	Located on the Continent
1. South Africa	_____
2. Czech Republic	_____
3. Nigeria	_____
4. Kenya	_____
5. Ukraine	_____
6. Iran	_____
7. Switzerland	_____
8. Australia	_____
9. Iraq	_____
10. Vietnam	_____
11. France	_____
12. Dem. Rep. of the Congo	_____
13. Russia	_____
14. Saudi Arabia	_____
15. Finland	_____
16. Israel	_____
17. Jordan	_____
18. Chad	_____
19. Myanmar	_____
20. Philippines	_____
21. India	_____
22. Denmark	_____
23. Egypt	_____
24. Afghanistan	_____
25. Sweden	_____

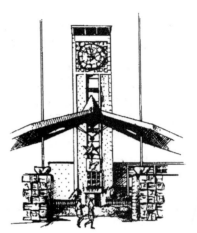

Kenyan parliament building in Nairobi

Name: _____ Date: _____

Unit 2: Population and Area in the Eastern Hemisphere

A. Population

The countries below are the 20 countries with the largest populations that lie completely in the Eastern Hemisphere. The population number is rounded. Using **Map 4** and **an atlas**, place the number on the map to locate each country.

1. China 1,339,000,000
2. India 1,185,000,000
3. Indonesia 234,000,000
4. Pakistan 170,000,000
5. Bangladesh 164,000,000
6. Nigeria 158,000,000
7. Russia 142,000,000
8. Japan 127,000,000
9. Philippines 94,000,000
10. Vietnam 86,000,000
11. Germany 85,000,000
12. Ethiopia 79,000,000
13. Egypt 79,000,000
14. Iran 75,000,000
15. Turkey 73,000,000
16. Democratic Republic of Congo 69,000,000
17. Thailand 64,000,000
18. Italy 60,000,000
19. Myanmar 50,000,000
20. South Africa 50,000,000

MAP 4

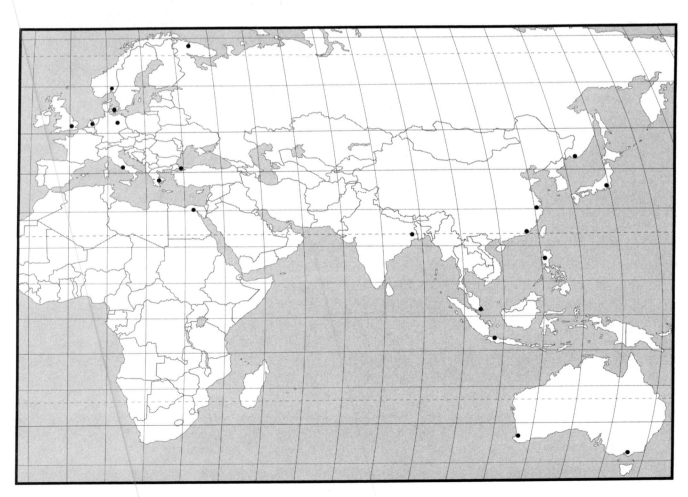

Name: _____   Date: _____

Unit 2: Population and Area in the Eastern Hemisphere

A. Population (cont.)

Use the population information from the previous page to answer the following questions.

1. The total population of China and India combined is   a) less than two billion
    b) more than two billion.

2. The total population of the other 18 countries combined is   a) less than two billion
    b) more than two billion.

3. Select the pie graph that best represents the comparison of populations between China and India and the other 18 countries. a) Pie Graph A   b) Pie Graph B

Pie Graph A

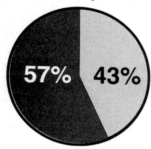

Pie Graph B

4. Write the name of the continent on which the country is located on the blank. If a country is located on two continents, write the name of the continent on which the capital city is located.

    a. China _____   b. India _____   c. Indonesia _____

    d. Russia _____   e. Pakistan _____   f. Bangladesh _____

    g. Japan _____   h. Nigeria _____   i. Germany _____

    j. Philippines _____   k. Vietnam _____   l. Egypt _____

    m. Turkey _____   n. Iran _____   o. Ethiopia _____

    p. Thailand _____   q. Italy _____   r. Dem. Rep. of Congo _____

    s. Myanmar _____   t. South Africa _____

5. Based on the population data for these 20 countries, place a plus (+) on the blank by the statement if it is a reasonable conclusion.

    ___ India and China are the two countries in the Eastern Hemisphere with the largest populations.

    ___ In population, India and China are approximately the same size.

    ___ The population of either India or China is much larger than any one of the other 18 countries.

Unit 2: Population and Area in the Eastern Hemisphere

A. Population (cont.)

Some of the largest cities of the Eastern Hemisphere are listed below with an approximate population. Complete the bar graph to compare the populations of the cities.

Tokyo 32,500,000
Cairo 14,500,000
Lagos 13,500,000
Karachi 12,000,000
Delhi 19,000,000
Paris 10,000,000
Tianjin 10,000,000

Seoul 21,000,000
Manila 16,500,000
Calcutta 15,000,000
London 13,000,000
Tehran 7,500,000
Dhaka 11,000,000
Bangkok 7,500,000

Mumbai 19,000,000
Moscow 15,000,000
Jakarta 19,000,000
Shanghai 17,000,000
Istanbul 9,500,000
Beijing 12,500,000
Hong Kong 6,000,000

City	0	2	4	6	8	10	12	14	16	18	20	22	24	26	28	30	32	34	36	38	40
Population in Millions																					
Tokyo																					
Seoul																					
Mumbai																					
Cairo																					
Manila																					
Moscow																					
Lagos																					
Calcutta																					
Jakarta																					
London																					
Shanghai																					
Delhi																					
Tehran																					
Istanbul																					
Paris																					
Dhaka																					
Beijing																					
Tianjin																					
Bangkok																					
Hong Kong																					

Name: _____   Date: _____

Unit 2: Population and Area in the Eastern Hemisphere

B. Area: Square kilometers

The areas in square kilometers for the 20 Eastern Hemisphere countries with the largest populations are listed below beside each country.

1. Russia 17,000,000
2. China 9,600,000
3. India 3,288,000
4. Dem. Rep. of Congo 2,345,000
5. Indonesia 1,919,000
6. Iran 1,648,000
7. South Africa 1,220,000
8. Ethiopia 1,127,000
9. Egypt 1,001,000
10. Nigeria 924,000
11. Pakistan 804,000
12. Turkey 781,000
13. Myanmar 679,000
14. Thailand 514,000
15. Japan 378,000
16. Germany 357,000
17. Vietnam 330,000
18. Italy 301,000
19. Philippines 300,000
20. Bangladesh 144,000

C. Population Density

In addition to knowing the population of a country, it is important to know how crowded the people are on the land. Density of population provides geographers with the number of people living on each square mile or kilometer.

To compute population density, divide the population by the land area. **Example:** Country A has an area of 500,000 square kilometers and a population of 5,000,000 people. 5,000,000 ÷ 500,000 = 10 persons per square kilometer.

1. Use the area information above and the population data from page 9 to complete the chart. Compute the population density using the formula **population ÷ area = population density**. Round the answer to the nearest whole person.

Country	Rank in Population	Rank in Area	Population Density
a. China	_____	_____	_____ per square kilometer
b. India	_____	_____	_____ per square kilometer
c. Indonesia	_____	_____	_____ per square kilometer
d. Russia	_____	_____	_____ per square kilometer
e. Pakistan	_____	_____	_____ per square kilometer
f. Bangladesh	_____	_____	_____ per square kilometer
g. Japan	_____	_____	_____ per square kilometer
h. Nigeria	_____	_____	_____ per square kilometer

Name: _____   Date: _____

Unit 2: Population and Area in the Eastern Hemisphere

C. Population Density (cont.)

Country	Rank in Population	Rank in Area	Population Density
i. Germany	_____	_____	_____ per square kilometer
j. Philippines	_____	_____	_____ per square kilometer
k. Vietnam	_____	_____	_____ per square kilometer
l. Egypt	_____	_____	_____ per square kilometer
m. Turkey	_____	_____	_____ per square kilometer
n. Iran	_____	_____	_____ per square kilometer
o. Thailand	_____	_____	_____ per square kilometer
p. Ethiopia	_____	_____	_____ per square kilometer
q. Italy	_____	_____	_____ per square kilometer
r. Myanmar	_____	_____	_____ per square kilometer
s. Dem. R. of Congo	_____	_____	_____ per square kilometer
t. South Africa	_____	_____	_____ per square kilometer

2. Which of the following is the most accurate statement (circle one)?

a) When studying a country, it is most important to know the area of the country.

b) When studying a country, it is most important to know the population size.

c) When studying a country, it is important to compare area and population.

A shantytown in New Delhi, India

Name: _____   Date: _____

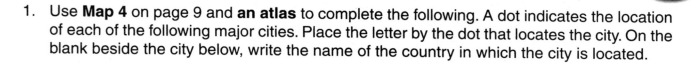

Unit 3: Cities of the Eastern Hemisphere

A. The Function of Cities

1. Use **Map 4** on page 9 and **an atlas** to complete the following. A dot indicates the location of each of the following major cities. Place the letter by the dot that locates the city. On the blank beside the city below, write the name of the country in which the city is located.

    a. London _____   b. Oslo _____   c. Rome _____

    d. Murmansk _____   e. Vladivostok _____   f. Berlin _____

    g. Istanbul _____   h. Athens _____   i. Amsterdam _____

    j. Copenhagen _____   k. Tokyo _____   l. Calcutta _____

    m. Alexandria _____   n. Hong Kong _____   o. Manila _____

    p. Singapore _____   q. Jakarta _____   r. Melbourne _____

    s. Shanghai _____   t. Perth _____

2. Use **Map 5** and **an atlas** to complete the following. A dot indicates the location of each of the following major cities. Place the letter by the dot that locates the city. On the blank beside the city below, write the name of the country in which the city is located.

    a. Budapest _____   b. Warsaw _____

    c. Moscow _____   d. Paris _____

    e. Cairo _____   f. Baghdad _____

    g. New Delhi _____   h. Mandalay _____

    i. Riyadh _____   j. Ulan Bator _____

    k. Tehran _____   l. Ankara _____

    m. Kano _____   n. Nairobi _____

A high-rise apartment building in Hong Kong, China

Name: _____ Date: _____

Unit 3: Cities of the Eastern Hemisphere

A. The Function of Cities (cont.)

MAP 5

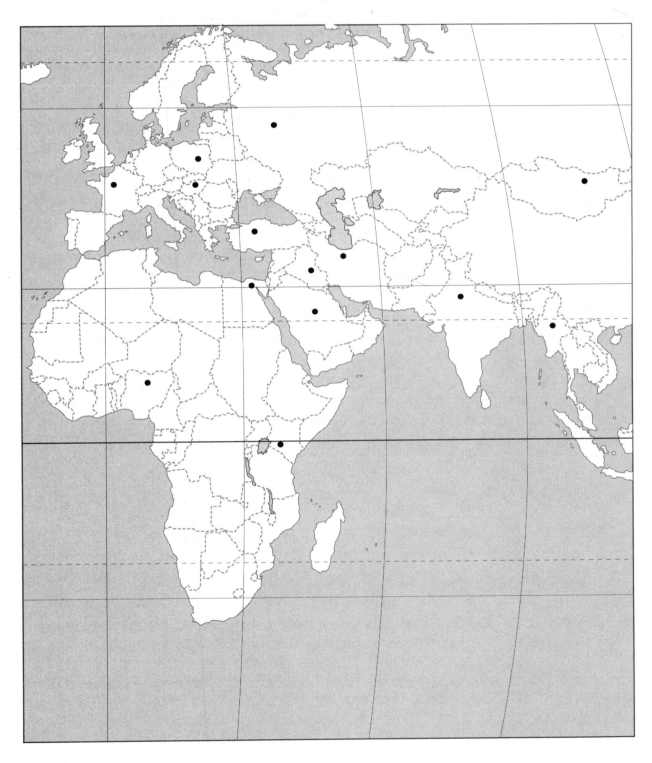

Name: _____ Date: _____

Unit 3: Cities of the Eastern Hemisphere

A. The Function of Cities (cont.)

Each city on Maps 4 and 5 is an important city in the country in which it is located. Each city serves many important functions within its country. The location of a city often determines its function. For example, a city may have been chosen to serve as a country's capital because its location provided safety from enemies. The city may function as the capital, as an important trading or manufacturing center, or as a financial and banking center.

3. Each of the following statements describes one of the cities below. The statement relates to the function of the city and why it is important. Read the statement and match the city to the statement. To complete the exercise, an atlas or map showing physical features and political boundaries will be necessary.

Paris	**Moscow**	**Berlin**	**Cape Town**	**Ankara**
London	**Kano**	**New Delhi**		

a. This city is located at the southernmost point on the African continent. In the sixteenth century, it was established as a supply station for Dutch trading ships that were sailing from Europe to India and the Far East.

    The city is   a) Paris   b) Ankara   c) Kano   d) Cape Town.

b. This city is the capital of a country that had been divided into two parts after World War II. The city itself was divided into east and west sections by a famous wall during the Cold War. Now the city is again the capital of a reunited country. This city is located on the North European Plain.

    The city is   a) Ankara   b) Berlin   c) New Delhi   d) Paris.

c. This city is located on an island that is part of Europe. It is a capital city, a port city, and also an important financial center. It was from this city that the country in which it is located once ruled an empire. British ships sailed to the American colonies from this port. The city is located on the Thames River.

    The city is   a) Moscow   b) Ankara   c) New Delhi   d) London.

d. This city is the capital of a country that spans two continents. It is a city that was first founded by explorers from the Scandinavian Peninsula. The explorers were traders who established a trading post and then followed the Volga River south to the Caspian Sea. The capital city is located deep inside the boundary of the country, and it has withstood invasions from Kublai Khan, Napoleon, and Hitler.

    The city is   a) Moscow   b) Ankara   c) New Delhi   d) London.

Name: _____ Date: _____

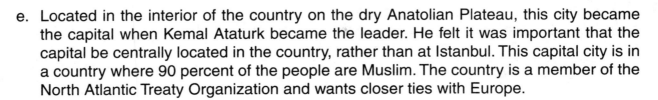

Unit 3: Cities of the Eastern Hemisphere

A. The Function of Cities (cont.)

e. Located in the interior of the country on the dry Anatolian Plateau, this city became the capital when Kemal Ataturk became the leader. He felt it was important that the capital be centrally located in the country, rather than at Istanbul. This capital city is in a country where 90 percent of the people are Muslim. The country is a member of the North Atlantic Treaty Organization and wants closer ties with Europe.

The city is   a) Moscow   b) Ankara   c) New Delhi   d) London.

f. This city is the capital of the country with the world's second-largest population. This beautiful city is located inland on the plain near the Ganges River. It was built by the British so the capital city would have a more central location with respect to the population of the country. The city, with its beautiful buildings and gardens, was designed and built to function as the capital city. Nearby is the large, crowded industrial city of Delhi.

The city is   a) Kano   b) Cape Town   c) Paris   d) New Delhi.

g. The country in which this city is located has the largest population in Africa. This city is located in the northern part of the country where most people are Muslim. In the southern part of the country, the majority of the people are Christian or practice a local religion. The city functions as an important trade and cultural center between other north African countries and the more densely populated cities in the southern part of the country.

The city is   a) Kano   b) Berlin   c) Paris   d) New Delhi.

h. Capital city, cultural center, financial center, and port city all could be used to describe this world-famous city. Located on the Seine River in Europe, this city, with its many monuments and beautiful buildings, is a tourist center.

The city is   a) Kano   b) Berlin   c) Paris
                  d) New Delhi.

Name: _____   Date: _____

Unit 3: Cities of the Eastern Hemisphere

A. Pretest Practice

Use an atlas to locate each city, and then fill in each blank to identify the country and the continent where the city is located.

1. The city Istanbul is located in _____ on the continent
    _____.

2. The city Oslo is located in _____ on the continent
    _____.

3. The city London is located in _____ on the continent
    _____.

4. The city Beijing is located in _____ on the continent _____.

5. The city Rome is located in _____ on the continent _____.

6. The city Shanghai is located in _____ on the continent _____.

7. The city Tokyo is located in _____ on the continent _____.

8. The city Calcutta is located in _____ on the continent _____.

9. The city Melbourne is located in _____ on the continent _____.

10. The city Jakarta is located in _____ on the continent _____.

11. The city Copenhagen is located in _____ on the continent _____.

12. The city Manila is located in _____ on the continent _____.

13. The city Kano is located in _____ on the continent _____.

14. The city Cairo is located in _____ on the continent _____.

15. The city Moscow is located in _____ on the continent _____.

16. The city Alexandria is located in _____ on the continent _____.

17. The city Budapest is located in _____ on the continent _____.

18. The city Bombay is located in _____ on the continent _____.

19. The city Seoul is located in _____ on the continent _____.

20. The city Karachi is located in _____ on the continent _____.

21. The city Bangkok is located in _____ on the continent _____.

22. The city St. Petersburg is located in _____ on the continent _____.

23. The city Paris is located in _____ on the continent _____.

24. The city Perth is located in _____ on the continent _____.

25. The city Berlin is located in _____ on the continent _____.

Name: _____ Date: _____

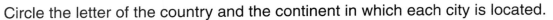

Unit 3: Cities of the Eastern Hemisphere

A. Test

Circle the letter of the country and the continent in which each city is located.

1. The city London is located in   a) England   b) Spain   c) Portugal   d) Russia
   on the continent   a) Asia   b) Africa   c) Australia   d) Europe.

2. The city Berlin is located in   a) England   b) Spain   c) Germany   d) Russia
   on the continent   a) Asia   b) Africa   c) Australia   d) Europe.

3. The city Shanghai is located in   a) China   b) India   c) Pakistan   d) Norway
   on the continent   a) Asia   b) Africa   c) Australia   d) Europe.

4. The city Calcutta is located in   a) China   b) India   c) Pakistan   d) Norway
   on the continent   a) Asia   b) Africa   c) Australia   d) Europe.

5. The city Melbourne is located in   a) Spain   b) Australia   c) South Africa   d) Sweden
   on the continent   a) Asia   b) Africa   c) Australia   d) Europe.

6. The city Copenhagen is located in   a) England   b) Denmark   c) Sweden   d) Iran
   on the continent   a) Asia   b) Africa   c) Australia   d) Europe.

7. The city Manila is located in   a) Indonesia   b) Philippines   c) Japan   d) India
   on the continent   a) Asia   b) Africa   c) Australia   d) Europe.

8. The city Kano is located in   a) India   b) Spain   c) Finland   d) Nigeria
   on the continent   a) Asia   b) Africa   c) Australia   d) Europe.

9. The city Cairo is located in   a) South Africa   b) Angola   c) Egypt   d) Iraq
   on the continent   a) Asia   b) Africa   c) Australia   d) Europe.

10. The city Moscow is located in   a) Russia   b) Hungary   c) Poland   d) Germany
    on the continent   a) Asia   b) Africa   c) Australia   d) Europe.

11. The city Budapest is located in   a) France   b) Slovakia   c) Hungary   d) Bulgaria
    on the continent   a) Asia   b) Africa   c) Australia   d) Europe.

12. The city Seoul is located in   a) North Korea   b) South Korea   c) China   d) Afghanistan
    on the continent   a) Asia   b) Africa   c) Australia   d) Europe.

13. The city Karachi is located in   a) Pakistan   b) Iran   c) India   d) Austria
    on the continent   a) Asia   b) Africa   c) Australia   d) Europe.

14. The city Bangkok is located in   a) Myanmar   b) Armenia   c) Vietnam   d) Thailand
    on the continent   a) Asia   b) Africa   c) Australia   d) Europe.

15. The city St. Petersburg is located in   a) France   b) Russia   c) Jordan   d) Israel
    on the continent   a) Asia   b) Africa   c) Australia   d) Europe.

Name: _____ Date: _____

Unit 4: Physical Features of the Eastern Hemisphere

A. Europe

1. Mountains

Each of the following mountain chains is located with a letter and the symbol △ on **Map 6**. Using **an atlas** and **Map 6**, locate the mountain chain, and circle the letter of the country or countries where the mountains are located.

Mountains	Country/Countries			
A. Jura	a) France	b) Germany	c) Italy	d) Switzerland
B. Alps	a) Switzerland	b) Italy	c) Poland	d) England
C. Apennines	a) Spain	b) Russia	c) Germany	d) Italy
D. Pyrenees	a) Spain	b) Russia	c) France	d) Italy
E. Carpathians	a) Romania	b) Italy	c) Poland	d) England
F. Urals	a) Spain	b) Russia	c) Germany	d) Italy
G. Caucasus	a) Georgia	b) Spain	c) Russia	d) England
H. Pennines	a) England	b) France	c) Germany	d) Italy
I. Kjolen	a) Norway	b) Denmark	c) Sweden	d) Bulgaria

MAP 6

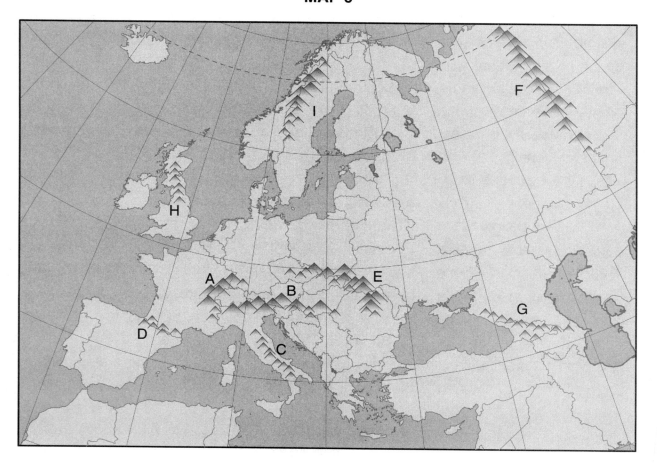

Name: _____ Date: _____

Unit 4: Physical Features of the Eastern Hemisphere

A. Europe (cont.)

2. Rivers

Each of the following rivers is located on **Map 7** with a letter. Using **an atlas** and **Map 7**, locate the river and circle the letter of the country or countries in which the river is located.

River	Country/Countries			
a. Thames	a) Poland	b) England	c) France	d) Germany
b. Seine	a) Poland	b) England	c) France	d) Germany
c. Rhône-Soane	a) Poland	b) England	c) France	d) Germany
d. Ebro	a) Italy	b) Germany	c) Poland	d) Spain
e. Po	a) Italy	b) Germany	c) Poland	d) Spain
f. Rhine	a) Italy	b) Germany	c) Poland	d) Spain
g. Danube	a) Romania	b) Bulgaria	c) Hungary	d) England
h. Vistula	a) Poland	b) Russia	c) Spain	d) France
i. Don	a) Poland	b) Russia	c) Spain	d) France
j. Tagus	a) Poland	b) Russia	c) Spain	d) France
k. Dneiper	a) Ukraine	b) Germany	c) Spain	d) France
l. Volga	a) Russia	b) Germany	c) Sweden	d) Czech Rep.

3. Plains

Each of the following plains is located on **Map 7** with a capital letter. Using **an atlas** and **Map 7**, locate the plain and circle the country or countries where the plain is located.

Plain	Country/Countries			
A. Hungarian	a) Romania	b) Bulgaria	c) Hungary	d) Germany
B. North European	a) Poland	b) Germany	c) Russia	d) Italy
C. Wallachian	a) Romania	b) France	c) Hungary	d) Germany

Unit 4: Physical Features of the Eastern Hemisphere

A. Europe (cont.)

MAP 7

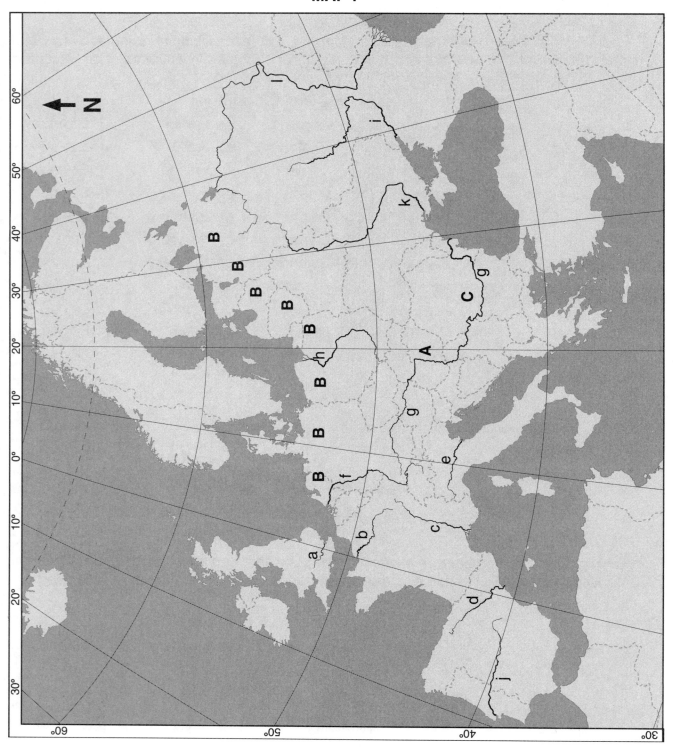

Name: _____ Date: _____

Unit 4: Physical Features of the Eastern Hemisphere

A. Europe (cont.)

4. Peninsulas

Use **Map 8** and **an atlas** to complete the following. Each of the countries below is located on a peninsula. Each peninsula is located with a capital letter. Circle the letter of the country or countries located on each peninsula.

Spain   **Italy**   **Norway**   **Sweden**   **Denmark**   **Portugal**

Peninsula		**Country/Countries**		
A. Iberian	a) Spain	b) Italy	c) Norway	d) Sweden
	e) Denmark	f) Portugal		
B. Jutland	a) Spain	b) Italy	c) Norway	d) Sweden
	e) Denmark	f) Portugal		
C. Scandinavian	a) Spain	b) Italy	c) Norway	d) Sweden
	e) Denmark	f) Portugal		
D. Italian	a) Spain	b) Italy	c) Norway	d) Sweden
	e) Denmark	f) Portugal		

5. Seas

Each of the following seas is located on Map 8 with a Roman numeral. Use **Map 8** and **an atlas** to identify each sea, and then circle the correct sea for each Roman numeral.

I.	a) Baltic	b) Mediterranean	c) Black	d) Aegean
	e) Adriatic	f) North		
II.	a) Baltic	b) Mediterranean	c) Black	d) Aegean
	e) Adriatic	f) North		
III.	a) Baltic	b) Mediterranean	c) Black	d) Aegean
	e) Adriatic	f) North		
IV.	a) Baltic	b) Mediterranean	c) Black	d) Aegean
	e) Adriatic	f) North		
V.	a) Baltic	b) Mediterranean	c) Black	d) Aegean
	e) Adriatic	f) North		
VI.	a) Baltic	b) Mediterranean	c) Black	d) Aegean
	e) Adriatic	f) North		

Name: _____ Date: _____

Unit 4: Physical Features of the Eastern Hemisphere

A. Europe (cont.)

MAP 8

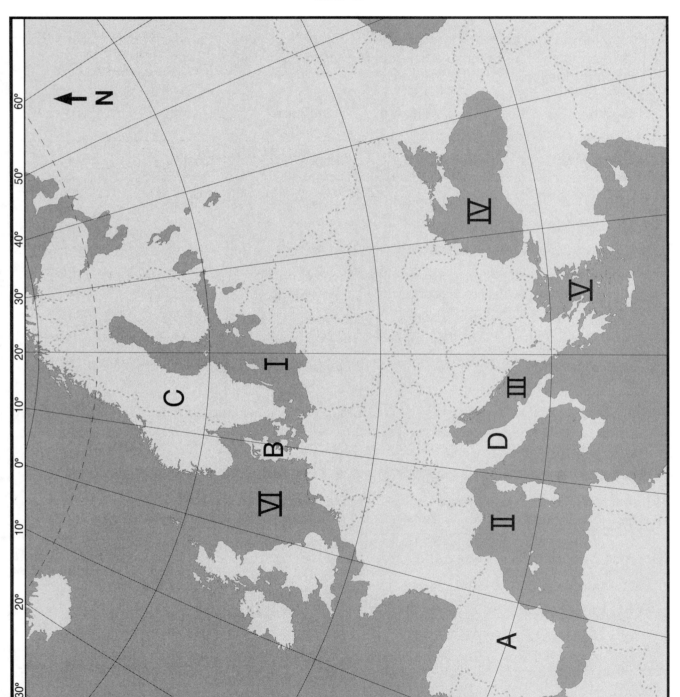

Name: _____   Date: _____

Unit 4: Physical Features of the Eastern Hemisphere

A. Europe—Pretest Practice

Use the terms below to fill in the blanks and complete each question.

Alps	**Thames**	**Baltic**	**Hungarian**	**Ebro**	**Rhine**	**Black**	**Pyrenees**
Urals	**Caucasus**	**Kjolen**	**Carpathians**	**Danube**	**Po**	**Wallachian**	
Iberian	**Jutland**	**Adriatic**	**Volga**	**Vistula**	**Seine**	**Mediterranean**	
Aegean	**Dneiper**	**North European**					

1. A famous river in England on which London is located is the _____.

2. The mountain chain on the border between Norway and Sweden is the _____.

3. This river in northern Italy flows across a fertile plain by the same name and into the Adriatic Sea. The river is the _____.

4. This large plain has made it easy for invading armies to move across northern Europe. The plain extends from the Netherlands, across northern Europe, and into Russia. This is the _____ Plain.

5. The mountains on the border between France and Spain are the _____.

6. This sea with many islands is located between Greece and Turkey. The sea is the _____.

7. Paris, the capital of France, is located on this river. The river is the _____.

8. The countries Denmark, Sweden, Poland, Lithuania, Latvia, and Estonia have ports on this sea. It is the _____ Sea.

9. A mountain chain in eastern Europe that extends through Poland, Slovakia, Ukraine, and Romania is the _____.

10. This sea is north of Turkey and south of the Ukraine. Ships must sail through the narrow Dardanelles and by Istanbul to enter this sea. It is the _____ Sea.

11. Denmark is located on the _____ Peninsula.

12. Spain and Portugal are located on the _____ Peninsula.

13. This famous river flows south across Russia into the Caspian Sea. This is the _____ River.

Name: _____   Date: _____

Unit 4: Physical Features of the Eastern Hemisphere

A. Europe—Pretest Practice (cont.)

14. These low mountains extending from north to south separate Europe from Asia. The mountains are the _____.

15. A river flowing by Kiev, south across the Ukraine, and into the Black Sea is the _____.

16. The sea located between Italy, Croatia, and Albania is the _____.

17. This river flows by Vienna, Budapest, and Belgrade and then along the border between Bulgaria and Romania into the Black Sea. It is the _____.

18. These mountains are found in Switzerland, Italy, Austria, and Germany. They are the _____.

19. This large fertile plain is found in Hungary. It is the _____ Plain.

20. This large fertile plain is found in Romania. It is the _____ Plain.

21. Around this sea, winters are mild and wet, while summers are hot and dry. Ships sailing from the Atlantic Ocean into this sea must sail through the Strait of Gibraltar. The sea is the _____.

22. These high mountains are found between the Caspian Sea and the Black Sea in the countries of Georgia and Azerbaijan. The mountains are the _____.

23. This river flows north across Poland by Warsaw and on to the Baltic Sea. This river is the _____.

24. This river located in northern Spain flows into the Mediterranean Sea. This river is the _____.

Name: _____   Date: _____

Unit 4: Physical Features of the Eastern Hemisphere

A. Europe—Test

Circle the letter of the correct answer.

1. A famous river in England on which London is located is the   a) Seine   b) Thames   c) Ebro   d) Danube.

2. This river in northern Italy flows across a fertile plain by the same name and into the Adriatic Sea. The river is the   a) Po   b) Danube   c) Vistula   d) Volga.

3. This large plain has made it easy for invading armies to move across northern Europe. This plain extends from the Netherlands, across northern Europe, and into Russia. This is the   a) Wallachian   b) North European   c) Hungarian   d) Ukrainian   Plain.

4. The mountains on the border between France and Spain are the   a) Pyrenees   b) Alps   c) Caucasus   d) Urals.

5. Paris, the capital of France, is located on this river. The river is the   a) Seine   b) Thames   c) Ebro   d) Danube.

6. The countries of Denmark, Sweden, Poland, Lithuania, Latvia, and Estonia have ports on the   a) Adriatic   b) Aegean   c) Mediterranean   d) Baltic Sea.

7. This sea is north of Turkey and south of the Ukraine. Ships must sail through the narrow Dardanelles and by Istanbul to enter this sea. It is the   a) Adriatic Sea   b) Aegean Sea   c) Baltic Sea   d) Black Sea.

8. Denmark is located on the   a) Iberian   b) Jutland   c) Italian   Peninsula.

9. This famous river flows south across Russia and into the Caspian Sea. This is the   a) Dneiper   b) Volga   c) Ebro   d) Vistula   River.

10. These low mountains extending from north to south separate Europe from Asia. The mountains are the   a) Alps   b) Caucasus   c) Urals   d) Pyrenees.

11. The sea located between Italy, Croatia, and Albania is the   a) Adriatic Sea   b) Aegean Sea   c) Baltic Sea   d) Black Sea.

12. This river flows by Vienna, Budapest, and Belgrade, then along the border between Bulgaria and Romania into the Black Sea. It is the a) Po b) Danube c) Vistula d) Volga.

13. These mountains are found in Switzerland, Italy, Austria, and Germany. They are the   a) Pyrenees   b) Caucasus   c) Alps   d) Urals.

14. Around this sea, winters are mild and wet, while summers are hot and dry. Ships sailing from the Atlantic Ocean into this sea must sail through the Strait of Gibraltar. The sea is the   a) Mediterranean   b) Aral   c) Black   d) Baltic.

15. These high mountains are found between the Caspian Sea and Black Sea in the countries of Georgia and Azerbaijan.   a) Pyrenees   b) Caucasus   c) Alps   d) Urals

Name: _____   Date: _____

Unit 4: Physical Features of the Eastern Hemisphere

B. Asia

1. Mountains

Each of the following mountain chains is located with a capital letter and symbol ▲ o n **Map 9**. Locate the mountain chain, and circle the letter of the country or countries where the mountains are located. Use an atlas, if necessary.

Mountains		**Country/Countries**		
A. Elburz	a) China	b) Turkey	c) Iran	d) Russia
B. Zagros	a) China	b) Turkey	c) Iran	d) Russia
C. Himalayas	a) India	b) Iran	c) Japan	d) Nepal
D. Tien Shan	a) China	b) Kyrgyzstan	c) Turkey	d) Nepal
E. Western Ghats	a) India	b) Iran	c) Japan	d) Nepal
F. Eastern Ghats	a) Iran	b) Japan	c) China	d) India

2. Rivers

Each of the following rivers is located on **Map 9** with a lowercase letter on the river. Locate the river and circle the letter of the country or countries in which the river is located. Use an atlas, if necessary.

River		**Country/Countries**		
a. Indus	a) Iran	b) Pakistan	c) China	d) Myanmar
b. Ganges	a) Philippines	b) Pakistan	c) India	d) Thailand
c. Tigris	a) Turkey	b) Russia	c) Iraq	d) India
d. Euphrates	a) Turkey	b) Russia	c) Iraq	d) India
e. Amur	a) China	b) Russia	c) South Korea	d) India
f. Mekong	a) Philippines	b) China	c) Vietnam	d) Cambodia
g . Irrawaddy	a) Iran	b) Pakistan	c) China	d) Myanmar
h. Yangtze (Chang)	a) Philippines	b) China	c) India	d) Thailand

Discovering the World of Geography: Grades 7–8   Unit 4: Physical Features—B. Asia

Name: _____ Date: _____

Unit 4: Physical Features of the Eastern Hemisphere

B. Asia (cont.)

MAP 9

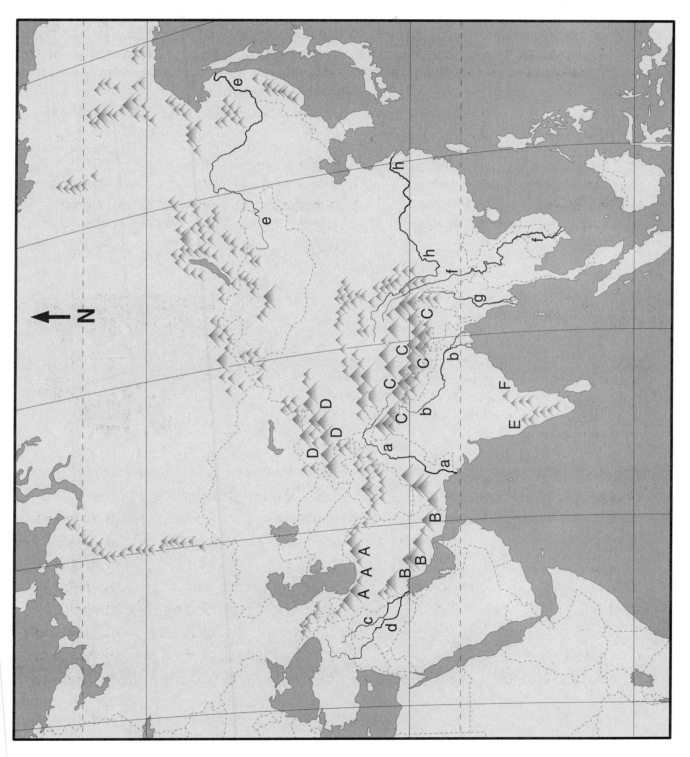

Name: _____ Date: _____

Unit 4: Physical Features of the Eastern Hemisphere

B. Asia (cont.)

3. Deserts

Each of the deserts listed below is located on **Map 10** with a capital letter inside the shaded area. To complete the exercise below, locate each desert, and circle the letter of the country or countries where the desert is located. Use an atlas, if necessary.

Desert	**Country/Countries**			
A. Gobi	a) Mongolia	b) India	c) Cambodia	d) Japan
B. Kyzylkum	a) China	b) India	c) Uzbekistan	d) Turkey
C. Takla Makan	a) India	b) Indonesia	c) China	d) Saudi Arabia
D. Karakum	a) Turkmenistan	b) Iraq	c) Jordan	d) Syria
E. Dasht-e Kavîr	a) Israel	b) Iran	c) India	d) Malaysia
F. Thar	a) Pakistan	b) India	c) Saudi Arabia	d) Mongolia
G. Nafud	a) Turkey	b) Israel	c) Saudi Arabia	d) Mongolia
H. Rub' al Khali	a) Syria	b) Israel	c) Mongolia	d) Saudi Arabia

MAP 10

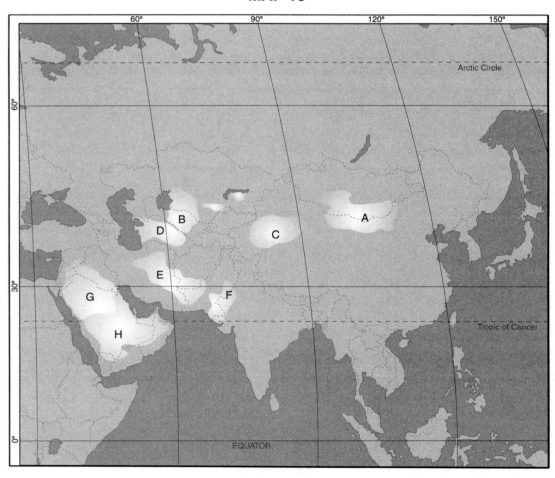

Name: _____   Date: _____

Unit 4: Physical Features of the Eastern Hemisphere

B. Asia (cont.)

4. Peninsulas

Use **Map 11** to complete the following. Each country is identified with a lowercase letter on the map. Place a + on the blank if the country is located on a peninsula.

___ a. Saudi Arabia   ___ b. Indonesia   ___ c. India   ___ d. Russia

___ e. Mongolia   ___ f. Malaysia   ___ g. Turkey   ___ h. Vietnam

___ i. Turkmenistan   ___ j. Thailand   ___ k. Japan   ___ l. South Korea

MAP 11

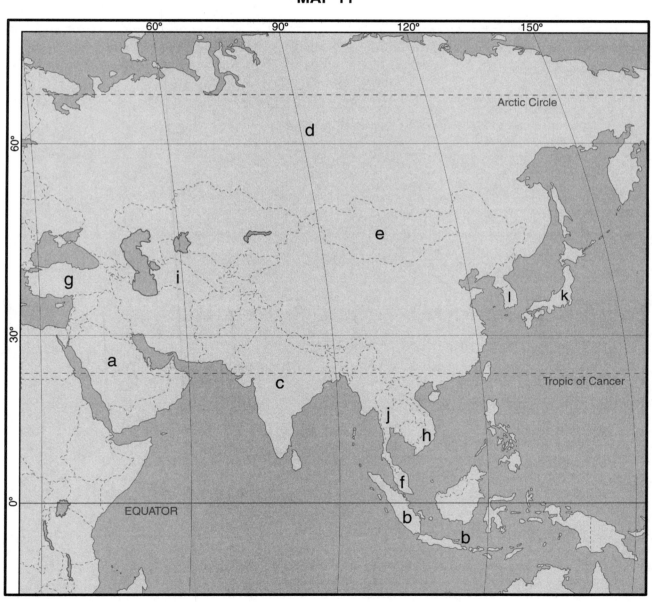

Name: _____ Date: _____

Unit 4: **Physical Features of the Eastern Hemisphere**

B. Asia (cont.)

5. Islands

Use **Map 12** to complete the following. Each country is located with a lowercase letter on the map. Place a plus (+) on the blank if the country is an island country.

__ a. Sri Lanka __ b. Afghanistan __ c. South Korea __ d. Philippines
__ e. Kazakhstan __ f. Indonesia __ g. Japan __ h. Iran
__ i. Myanmar __ j. Taiwan

MAP 12

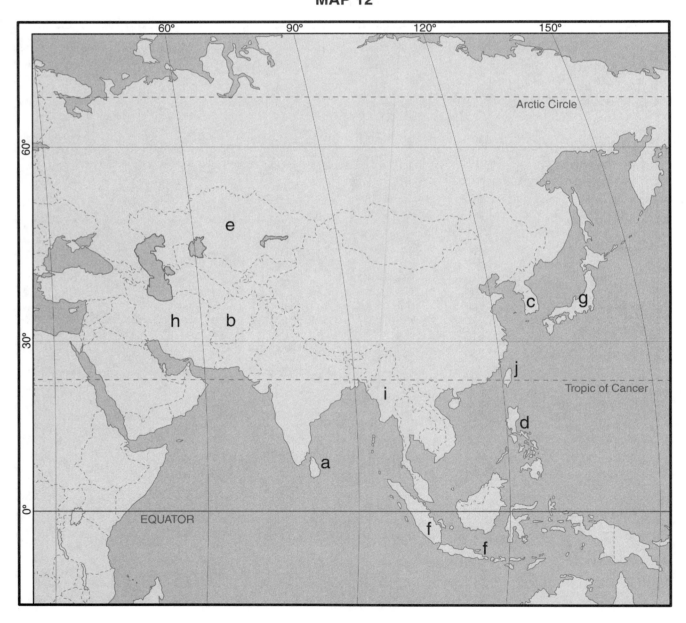

Name: _____ Date: _____

Unit 4: Physical Features of the Eastern Hemisphere

B. Asia (cont.)

6. Seas

Each of the following seas is located on **Map 13** with a Roman numeral. Using **Map 13** and **an atlas**, circle the letter of the correct answer below for each Roman numeral on the map.

Sea

I. a) Red Sea   b) Arabian Sea   c) South China Sea   d) Sea of Japan
    e) Sea of Okhotsk   f) Bering Sea   g) Black Sea   h) Aral Sea   i) Caspian Sea

II. a) Red Sea   b) Arabian Sea   c) South China Sea   d) Sea of Japan
    e) Sea of Okhotsk   f) Bering Sea   g) Black Sea   h) Aral Sea   i) Caspian Sea

III. a) Red Sea   b) Arabian Sea   c) South China Sea   d) Sea of Japan
    e) Sea of Okhotsk   f) Bering Sea   g) Black Sea   h) Aral Sea   i) Caspian Sea

IV. a) Red Sea   b) Arabian Sea   c) South China Sea   d) Sea of Japan
    e) Sea of Okhotsk   f) Bering Sea   g) Black Sea   h) Aral Sea   i) Caspian Sea

V. a) Red Sea   b) Arabian Sea   c) South China Sea   d) Sea of Japan
    e) Sea of Okhotsk   f) Bering Sea   g) Black Sea   h) Aral Sea   i) Caspian Sea

VI. a) Red Sea   b) Arabian Sea   c) South China Sea   d) Sea of Japan
    e) Sea of Okhotsk   f) Bering Sea   g) Black Sea   h) Aral Sea   i) Caspian Sea

VII. a) Red Sea   b) Arabian Sea   c) South China Sea   d) Sea of Japan
    e) Sea of Okhotsk   f) Bering Sea   g) Black Sea   h) Aral Sea   i) Caspian Sea

VIII. a) Red Sea   b) Arabian Sea   c) South China Sea   d) Sea of Japan
    e) Sea of Okhotsk   f) Bering Sea   g) Black Sea   h) Aral Sea   i) Caspian Sea

IX. a) Red Sea   b) Arabian Sea   c) South China Sea   d) Sea of Japan
    e) Sea of Okhotsk   f) Bering Sea   g) Black Sea   h) Aral Sea   i) Caspian Sea

7. Plateaus

On **Map 13**, plateaus are located using the symbol ⌢ over a capital letter. Using **Map 13** and **an atlas**, locate each plateau, and circle the letter of the country/region where the plateau is located.

Plateau	Country/Region			
A. Deccan Plateau	a) Iran	b) India	c) China	d) Tibet
B. Tibetan Plateau	a) Tibet	b) India	c) Thailand	d) Afghanistan
C. Plateau of Iran	a) Iran	b) India	c) China	d) Tibet

Name: _____ Date: _____

Unit 4: Physical Features of the Eastern Hemisphere

B. Asia (cont.)

MAP 13

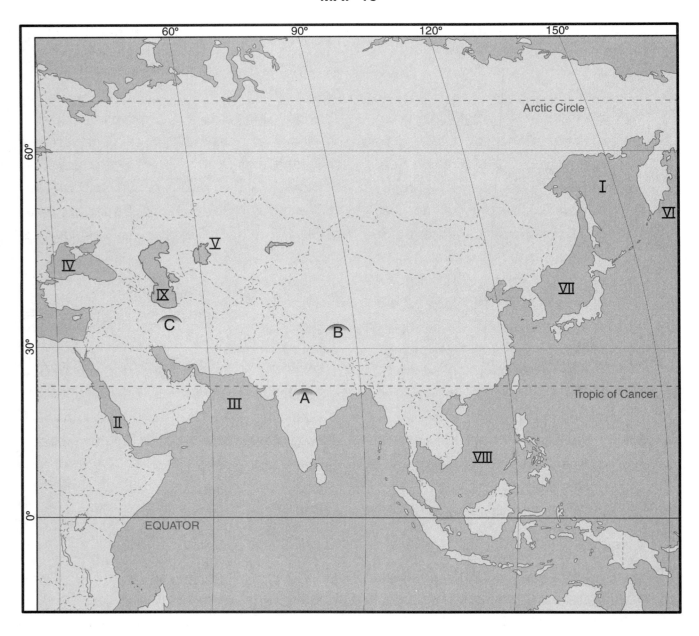

Name: _____   Date: _____

Unit 4: Physical Features of the Eastern Hemisphere

B. Asia—Pretest Practice

Use the terms below to complete each statement.

Himalayas	Indus	Arabian Sea	Tigris	Ganges	Tien Shan	Euphrates
Western Ghats		Eastern Ghats	Elburz	Irrawaddy	Kyzylkum	Takla Makan
Yangtze	Amur	Thar	Caspian	Karakum	Huang Ho	Red Sea
South China Sea		Aral Sea				

1. These mountains are located in Iran at the southern end of the Caspian Sea. They are the _____.

2. This important river located in Pakistan flows south into the Arabian Sea. The river is the _____.

3. This desert is located in the Central Asian country of Uzbekistan near the Aral Sea. The desert is the _____.

4. This river flows south from Mandalay in Myanmar to Rangoon and into the Bay of Bengal. The river is the _____.

5. Nepal is located in these high mountains between China and India. Here, at over 29,000 feet, is located Mt. Everest. The mountains are the _____.

6. This desert is located in the Central Asian country Turkmenistan. It is the _____.

7. This river flows across the North China Plain into the Yellow Sea. It is also known as the Yellow River. Levees to control flooding often break and cause great damage to the surrounding communities. The river is the _____.

8. This desert, located on the Pakistani and Indian border, is also known as the Great Indian Desert. The desert is the _____ Desert.

9. This desert is located in the Tarim Basin between the Tien Shan and Altun Shan Mountains in westernmost China. It is the _____ Desert.

Name: _____   Date: _____

Unit 4: Physical Features of the Eastern Hemisphere

B. Asia—Pretest Practice (cont.)

10. These mountains are located on the western and eastern coasts of India. The mountains are the _____ and _____.

11. This famous river in northern India has special religious significance to Hindus. Many Hindus make pilgrimages to bathe in this river, which flows into the Bay of Bengal. The river is the _____.

12. The Volga River flows into this landlocked sea. The sea is the _____ Sea.

13. Located in Mongolia and China, this is a world-famous desert. It is the _____ Desert.

14. This sea is located on the border of Uzbekistan and Kazakhstan. The Syr Darya and Amu Darya rivers flow into this landlocked sea. Water has been taken from the rivers to irrigate the nearby desert land for crops. Because less water enters the sea due to this irrigation, the sea has been shrinking in size. The sea is the _____ Sea.

15. These rivers are located in Iraq. The rivers flow south across Iraq through a region once known as Mesopotamia and into the Persian Gulf. The rivers are the _____ and _____.

16. This river flows east through central China into the East China Sea near Shanghai. The river is the _____.

17. East of Oman, south of Pakistan, and west of India is this famous sea. It is the _____ Sea.

18. This river flows along the border of Russia and Manchuria in China. It flows into the Sea of Japan near the port city of Vladivostok. The river is the _____.

19. This sea is located between Saudi Arabia and Egypt. Ships sail this sea to get from the Mediterranean Sea to the Indian Ocean. The sea is the _____ Sea.

20. This sea is located between Vietnam and the Philippines. It is the _____ Sea.

Name: _____　Date: _____

Unit 4: Physical Features of the Eastern Hemisphere

B. Asia—Test

Circle the letter of the correct answer.

1. These mountains are located in Iran at the south-ern end of the Caspian Sea. They are the
   a) Tien Shan　b) Himalayas　c) Elburz
   d) Eastern Ghats.

2. This important river located in Pakistan flows south into the Arabian Sea. The river is the　a) Ganges　b) Indus　c) Irrawaddy　d) Huang Ho.

3. This desert is located in the Central Asian country of Uzbekistan near the Aral Sea. The desert is the a) Kyzylkum　b) Karakum　c) Thar　d) Gobi.

4. This river flows south from Mandalay in Myanmar to Rangoon and into the Bay of Bengal. The river is the a) Ganges　b) Indus　c) Irrawaddy　d) Huang Ho.

5. These high mountains between China and India are located in Nepal, where Mt. Everest can be found. The mountains are the　a) Tien Shan　b) Himalayas　c) Elburz.

6. This river flows across the North China Plain into the Yellow Sea. It is also known as the Yellow River. The river is the　a) Ganges　b) Indus　c) Irrawaddy　d) Huang Ho.

7. This desert is located in the Tarim Basin between the Tien Shan and Altun Shan Mountains in westernmost China. It is the　a) Thar　b) Takla Makan　c) Gobi　d) Karakum.

8. These mountains are located on the eastern coast of India. The mountains are the
   a) Western Ghats　b) Eastern Ghats　c) Tien Shan　d) Elburz.

9. This famous river in northern India that flows into the Bay of Bengal has special significance to Hindus. The river is the　a) Indus　b) Huang Ho　c) Irrawaddy　d) Ganges.

10. The Volga River flows into this sea. The sea is the　a) Aral　b) Caspian　c) Arabian
    d) South China Sea.

11. Located in Mongolia and China, this is a world-famous desert. It is the　a) Thar
    b) Karakum　c) Kyzylkum　d) Gobi　　　　Desert.

12. This sea is located on the border of Uzbekistan and Kazakhstan. The Syr Darya and Amu Darya Rivers flow into this landlocked sea. The sea is the　a) Caspian　b) Arabian
    c) Aral　d) Yellow Sea

13. These rivers flow south across Iraq through a region once known as Mesopotamia and into the Persian Gulf. The rivers are the a) Yangtze and Huang Ho　b) Indus and Ganges
    c) Irrawaddy and Amur　d) Tigris and Euphrates.

14. This river flows east through central China into the East China Sea near Shanghai. The river is the　a) Yangtze　b) Huang Ho　c) Amur　d) Irrawaddy.

15. This sea is located between Saudi Arabia and Egypt and is a route for ships to get from the Mediterranean Sea to the Indian Ocean. This is the　a) Aral　b) Arabian　c) Red　Sea.

Name: _____   Date: _____

Unit 4: Physical Features of the Eastern Hemisphere

C. Africa

1. Mountains

On **Map 14**, each of the following mountain chains is indicated by a capital letter. Individual mountain peaks are located with a capital letter under the symbol ∧. Using **Map 14** and **an atlas**, locate the mountain chain or individual mountain, and circle the letter of the country or countries where each is located.

A. Atlas	a) Morocco	b) Egypt	c) Algeria	d) Sudan
B. Drakensberg	a) South Africa	b) Liberia	c) Nigeria	d) Angola
C. Mt. Kilimanjaro	a) Kenya	b) Tanzania	c) Zambia	d) Namibia
D. Mt. Kenya	a) Kenya	b) Tanzania	c) Zambia	d) Namibia
E. Ruwenzori	a) Zambia	b) Uganda	c) Mali	d) Somalia

2. Rivers

Each of the following rivers is indicated on **Map 14** by a lowercase letter. Using **Map 14** and **an atlas**, locate each river, and circle the letter of the country or countries in which the river is located.

a. Nile	a) Niger	b) Egypt	c) Mozambique	d) Ghana
b. Congo	a) Dem. Rep. of Congo	b) Liberia	c) Senegal	d) Togo
c. Orange	a) South Africa	b) Sudan	c) Namibia	d) Ghana
d. Niger	a) Mali	b) Tanzania	c) Niger	d) Nigeria
e. Benue	a) Mali	b) Tanzania	c) Niger	d) Nigeria
f. Zambezi	a) Zimbabwe	b) Gabon	c) Zambia	d) Mozambique
g. Limpopo	a) Botswana	b) South Africa	c) Mozambique	d) Gabon

3. Deserts

Each of the following deserts is indicated on **Map 14** by a number. Using **Map 14** and **an atlas**, locate each desert, and circle the letter of the country or countries where the desert is located.

1. Sahara	a) Mali	b) Egypt	c) Namibia	d) Sudan
2. Namib	a) Mali	b) Egypt	c) Namibia	d) Libya
3. Libyan	a) Mali	b) Egypt	c) Namibia	d) Libya
4. Kalahari	a) Zambia	b) Botswana	c) Kenya	d) Togo

Name: _____ Date: _____

Unit 4: Physical Features of the Eastern Hemisphere

C. Africa (cont.)

4. Lakes

On **Map 14**, lakes are indicated by the symbol ⬭ and a number on or near the symbol. Using **Map 14** and **an atlas**, locate each lake. Circle the letter of the country or countries in which the lake is located.

1. Lake Chad   a) Niger   b) Sudan   c) Chad   d) Benin
2. Lake Victoria   a) Uganda   b) Kenya   c) Tanzania   d) Senegal
3. Lake Tanganyika a) Tanzania b) Kenya   c) Dem. Rep. of Congo d) Sierra Leone
4. Lake Albert   a) Tanzania b) Kenya   c) Dem. Rep. of Congo   d) Uganda
5. Lake Nyasa   a) Malawi   b) Ethiopia   c) Mozambique   d) Zambia

5. Great Rift Valley

In eastern Africa, Lake Albert, Lake Tanganyika, and Lake Nyasa are long, slender lakes. All of these lakes are part of the Great Rift Valley. In this region, the lakes are on the floor of the Great Rift Valley. This valley was formed many millions of years ago. See the diagram below. Use **an atlas or wall map of Africa**, and place a + on the blank if the Great Rift Valley is found in the country.

____ Chad   ____ Liberia   ____ Tanzania   ____ Kenya   ____ Zambia
____ Democratic Republic of the Congo   ____ Malawi   ____ Madagascar

DIAGRAM 1

Name: _____ Date: _____

Unit 4: Physical Features of the Eastern Hemisphere

C. Africa (cont.)

MAP 14

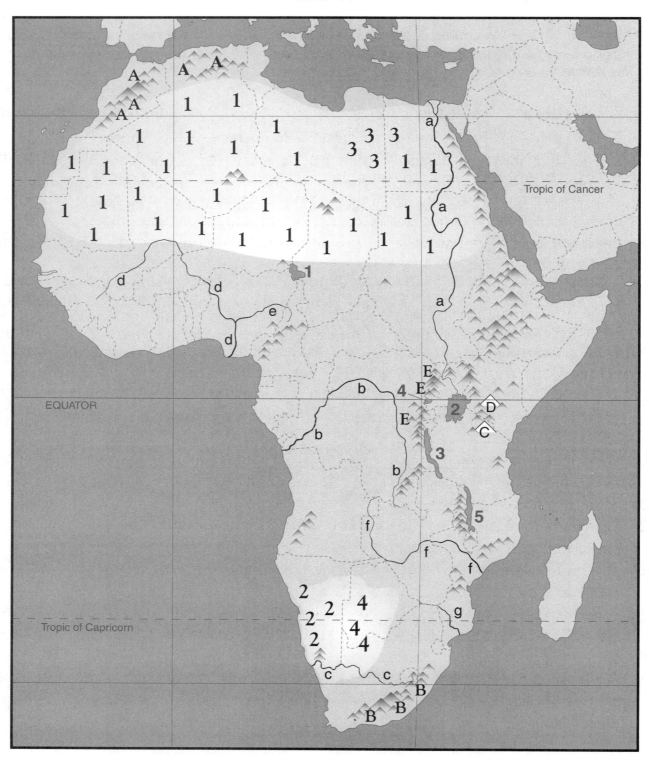

Unit 4: Physical Features of the Eastern Hemisphere

C. Africa—Pretest Practice

Use the terms below to fill in the blanks and complete each question.

Atlas	**Lake Victoria**	**Lake Tanganyika**	**Sahara**	**Zambezi**
Congo	**Drakensberg**	**Great Rift Valley**	**Nile**	**Kalahari**
Mt. Kenya	**Lake Chad**	**Mt. Kilimanjaro**		

1. This large lake, which was named after an English queen, is located on the equator on the border between Kenya and Tanzania. The lake is _____.

2. One of two very famous African mountain peaks, it is located in Tanzania just south of the border with Kenya. The mountain peak is _____.

3. This lake is located in the Great Rift Valley on the border between Tanzania and the Democratic Republic of the Congo. It is _____.

4. Beginning in Uganda and Ethiopia, this famous river flows north through Egypt to the Mediterranean Sea at Alexandria. The river is the _____.

5. Located in the tropics, this river flows west through the heavily forested Democratic Republic of the Congo. Near Brazzaville, the river drops down to the coastal area and flows into the Atlantic Ocean. The river is the _____.

6. This lake is located on the southern fringe of the Sahara Desert. It is located on the border between Nigeria and Chad. The lake is _____.

7. This desert, located in Botswana, is the home of the Hottentots. The Hottentots are nomadic people who have learned to survive in this very dry desert. The desert is the

_____.

8. Located near the center of Kenya, this volcanic mountain peak is the highest in Kenya. The mountain peak is   _____.

9. Found in Morocco and Algeria is a mountain chain called the _____ Mountains.

10. Along the southeast coast of South Africa is a mountain range called the _____ Mountains.

11. This river flows along the boundary of Zambia and Zimbabwe, east across Mozambique. The river is the _____.

12. This long valley extends along the eastern side of Africa. On the floor of the valley are the long, slender lakes of Lake Tanganyika, Lake Nyasa, and Lake Albert. It is called the

_____.

13. This large desert in Africa, located north of the equator, is the world's largest desert. It is the home of the veiled Tuareg tribe. Niger, Chad, Egypt, Libya, Sudan, and Mali all have territory in this desert. The desert is the _____.

Unit 4: Physical Features of the Eastern Hemisphere

C. Africa—Test

Circle the letter of the correct answer.

1. This large lake, which was named after an English queen, is located on the equator on the border between Kenya and Tanzania. The lake is Lake   a) Tanganyika   b) Albert   c) Nyasa   d) Victoria.

2. One of two very famous African mountain peaks, it is located in Tanzania near the border with Kenya. The mountain peak is   a) Mt. Kilimanjaro   b) Mt. Everest   c) Mt. Kenya.

3. This lake is located in the Great Rift Valley on the border between Tanzania and the Democratic Republic of the Congo. Like other lakes in the Great Rift Valley, it is a long and slender lake. It is Lake   a) Tanganyika   b) Albert   c) Nyasa   d) Victoria.

4. Beginning in Uganda and Ethiopia, this famous river flows north through Egypt to the Mediterranean Sea at Alexandria. The river is the   a) Nile   b) Niger   c) Congo.

5. Located in the tropics, this river flows west through the heavily forested Democratic Republic of the Congo. Near Brazzaville, the river drops down to the coastal area and flows into the Atlantic Ocean. The river is the   a) Nile   b) Niger   c) Zambezi   d) Congo.

6. This lake is located on the southern fringe of the Sahara Desert. It is located on the border between Nigeria and Chad. The lake is   a) Lake Kenya   b) Lake Chad   c) Lake Victoria   d) Lake Albert.

7. This desert, located in Botswana, is the home of the nomadic people called the Hottentots. The desert is the   a) Kalahari   b) Namib   c) Sahara   d) Libyan.

8. This volcanic peak is the highest in Kenya. The mountain peak is   a) Mt. Kilimanjaro   b) Mt. Everest   c) Mt. Kenya.

9. This mountain chain is found in Morocco and Algeria. It is the   a) Drakensberg   b) Ruwenzori   c) Atlas   Mountains.

10. This mountain chain is located along the southeast coast of South Africa. The mountain chain is the   a) Drakensberg   b) Ruwenzori   c) Atlas.

11. This river flows along the boundary of Zambia and Zimbabwe, east across Mozambique. The river is the   a) Congo   b) Niger   c) Zambezi   d) Nile.

12. This long valley extends along the eastern side of Africa. On the floor of the valley are the long, slender lakes of Lake Tanganyika, Lake Nyasa, and Lake Albert. The valley is the   a) Tanganyika   b) Malawi   c) Rwanda   d) Great Rift   Valley.

13. This large desert in Africa, located north of the equator, is the world's largest desert. It is the home of the veiled Tuareg tribe. Niger, Chad, Egypt, Libya, Sudan, and Mali all have territory in this desert. The desert is the   a) Kalahari   b) Namib   c) Sahara   d) Libyan.

Name: _____ Date: _____

Unit 4: Physical Features of the Eastern Hemisphere

D. Australia

Use **Map 15** and **an atlas** to complete the following. The following symbols are used on Map 15.

Mountains   Desert   River   Reef

1. The continent of Australia has only one country; it is also named Australia. Australia is divided into the following political divisions. Write the name of each political division on Map 15 in the correct location.

   a) Western Australia   b) Northern Territory   c) South Australia   d) Queensland
   e) New South Wales   f) Victoria   g) Tasmania

Circle the letter of the correct answer.

2. The Great Dividing Range is located using the symbol [symbol]. The Great Dividing Range is located in   a) Western Australia   b) Queensland   c) Northern Territory
   d) New South Wales.

3. The Darling River is located in   a) Western Australia   b) South Australia
   c) Northern Territory   d) New South Wales.

4. The Murray River is located in   a) Victoria   b) New South Wales   c) Northern Territory
   d) Western Australia.

5. The Great Sandy Desert is located in   a) Victoria   b) New South Wales
   c) Northern Territory   d) Western Australia.

6. The Great Victoria Desert is located in   a) Victoria   b) South Australia
   c) Northern Territory   d) Western Australia.

7. The Gibson Desert is located in   a) Victoria   b) New South Wales
   c) Northern Territory   d) Western Australia.

8. Located southeast of Australia is a small island country. The country is located on two islands. One is North Island and the other South Island. The country is   a) Indonesia
   b) New Zealand   c) India   d) the Philippines.

9. Located to the north of Australia is another country composed of hundreds of islands. The island country is   a) Indonesia   b) New Zealand   c) India   d) the Philippines.

10. The Great Barrier Reef is the world's largest coral reef. Locate and label it on the map.

Name: _____　Date: _____

Unit 4: Physical Features of the Eastern Hemisphere

D. Australia

MAP 15

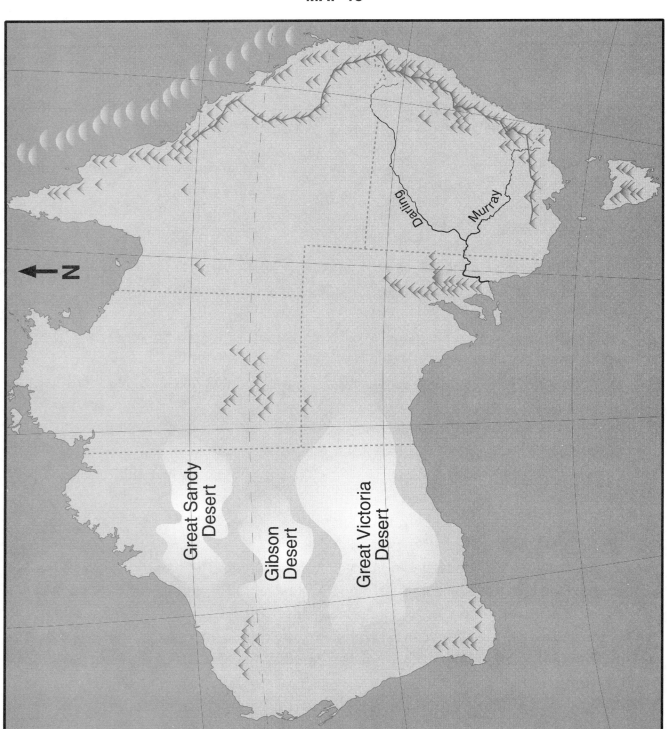

Name: _____   Date: _____

Unit 4: Physical Features of the Eastern Hemisphere

D. Australia—Pretest Practice

Write the correct term from the list below on each blank to answer the question.

New Zealand   **Great Dividing Range**   **Darling**   **Great Victoria**   **Murray**
Gibson   **Great Barrier Reef**   **Indonesia**   **Tasmania**   **Australia**
Great Sandy   **Western Australia**

1. The mountain range found in eastern Australia is the _____.

2. The river that flows south across New South Wales and into the Indian Ocean near Adelaide

    is the _____.

3. The Great Victoria, Great Sandy, and Gibson Deserts are found in the province of

    _____.

4. The only country located on the continent of Australia is _____.

5. Located off the southeast coast of Australia in the Pacific Ocean is a small country made up of

    two main islands, North Island and South Island. The country is _____.

6. The island province in Australia is _____.

7. The island country located north of Australia is _____.

8. The three deserts found in Western Australia are the _____,

    _____, and _____.

9. The river that forms a border between Victoria and New South Wales is the _____.

10. The largest coral reef in the world is the _____.

Name: _____ Date: _____

Unit 4: Physical Features of the Eastern Hemisphere

D. Australia—Test

Circle the letter of the correct answer.

Harbor in Auckland, New Zealand

1. The mountain range found in eastern Australia is

    the   a) Alps   b) Caucasus

    c) Great Dividing Range   d) Drakensberg.

2. The river that flows south across New South Wales

    and into the Indian Ocean near Adelaide is the   a) Ganges   b) Darling

    c) Huang Ho   d) Rhine.

3. The Great Victoria, Great Sandy, and Gibson Deserts are found in the province of

    a) Western Australia   b) New South Wales   c) Queensland   d) Victoria.

4. The only country located on the continent of Australia is   a) New Zealand   b) Indonesia

    c) Australia   d) Tasmania.

5. Located off the southeast coast of Australia in the Pacific Ocean is a small country made

    up of two main islands, North Island and South Island. The country is   a) New Zealand

    b) Indonesia   c) Australia   d) Tasmania.

6. The island province in Australia is   a) New South Wales   b) Western Australia

    c) Queensland   d) Tasmania

7. The island country located north of Australia is   a) New Zealand   b) Indonesia

    c) Australia   d) Tasmania.

8. The three deserts found in Western Australia are the   a) Sahara, Namib, and Kalahari

    b) Gibson, Great Victoria, and Great Sandy   c) Gobi, Takla Makan, and Thar.

9. The river that forms a border between Victoria and New South Wales is the   a) Darling

    b) Nile   c) Murray   d) Fitzroy.

10. The largest coral reef in the world is the   a) Bikini Atoll   b) Great Barrier Reef

    c) Caribbean Reef.

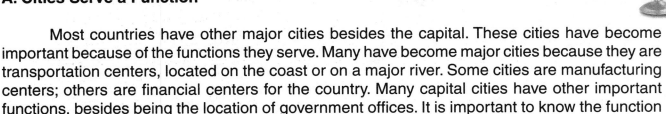

Unit 5: More About the Function of Cities

A. Cities Serve a Function

Most countries have other major cities besides the capital. These cities have become important because of the functions they serve. Many have become major cities because they are transportation centers, located on the coast or on a major river. Some cities are manufacturing centers; others are financial centers for the country. Many capital cities have other important functions, besides being the location of government offices. It is important to know the function of major cities when studying a country.

1. Cities in Europe

Use **a wall map** or **an atlas** that shows the political and physical features and major cities for countries in Europe. From the description below, identify the city and name the country in which it is located. Also, place a plus sign (+) under the major functions of the city.

a. This capital city is the capital of the second-largest country in Europe. During the Colonial period, Benjamin Franklin, John Adams, and Thomas Jefferson spent many years here trying to gain the country's support in the fight for independence. It is also a noted tourist attraction with many beautiful gardens. Tourists from all over the world come to this city, as it is a cultural center with beautiful buildings, gardens, and works of art. Located on the Seine River in the midst of a fertile farming region, it is an important transportation center. The country in which the city is located has port cities on the Atlantic Ocean and Mediterranean Sea.

The city is   a) Budapest   b) Copenhagen   c) Paris   d) Berlin.

It is located in _____.

Government	Transportation	Tourist	Finance	Trade	Manufacturing
_____	_____	_____	_____	_____	_____

b. This city is located on a peninsula along the Mediterranean coast. It is a capital city and the location of the Vatican. In addition to being a capital, it is an important tourist center, as people come here from all over the world to worship and see the great cathedrals. It also boasts works of art, museums, and ancient ruins.

This city is   a) Naples   b) Rome   c) Bologna   d) Warsaw.

It is located in _____.

Government	Transportation	Tourist	Finance	Trade	Manufacturing
_____	_____	_____	_____	_____	_____

Name: _____ Date: _____

Unit 5: More About the Function of Cities

A. Cities Serve a Function—Cities in Europe (cont.)

c. It is a port city on the Adriatic Sea and was settled on a lagoon with many islands. The settlers chose this location in the fifth and sixth centuries to escape the barbarians who were raiding the country. Protected from invaders by the marshy lagoon location at the mouth of the Po River, the city developed as a financial and commercial center where traders and explorers could find individuals who would loan them money for their ventures. In fact, it was from here that traders like Marco Polo set out for the Far East. The city is also well known for its glass manufacturing. Today, it is a prosperous commercial and trading center.

The city is   a) Rome   b) Paris   c) Warsaw   d) Venice.

It is located in _____.

Government   Transportation   Tourist   Finance   Trade   Manufacturing

_____   _____   _____   _____   _____   _____

d. This city is located in the Ruhr region of Europe and is an important industrial and transportation center. It is located near the Rhine River, one of Europe's most famous rivers. There are many castles and beautiful hillside vineyards nearby. Located in the Ruhr region where iron and coal deposits were once mined, it became an industrial city, producing heavy equipment. Even though the iron and coal deposits in the Ruhr have been exhausted, it has remained a major manufacturing center of heavy machinery and equipment by importing the needed iron and coal.

The city is   a) Berlin   b) Munich   c) Essen   d) Vienna.

It is located in _____.

Government   Transportation   Tourist   Finance   Trade   Manufacturing

_____   _____   _____   _____   _____   _____

Name: _____   Date: _____

Unit 5: More About the Function of Cities

A. Cities Serve a Function—Cities in Europe (cont.)

e. Located on the North European Plain, this city is the capital and largest city of the country in which it is located. It is one of the country's major industrial centers, producing steel and heavy equipment. The city is an important transportation center on the Vistula River.

The city is   a) Gdansk   b) Warsaw   c) Prague   d) Minsk.

It is located in _____.

Government	Transportation	Tourist	Finance	Trade	Manufacturing
___	___	___	___	___	___

f. This capital city, located on the Danube River, is the major city in the country and is also the largest. Because the country is landlocked, its location on one of Europe's major rivers is very important. The country in which the city is located is home to the Magyars. Because of the rich, long history dating from Roman occupation to the present, many tourists come here to see the museums, monuments, and churches. In addition to being the home of government offices, the city is a transportation center for agricultural crops produced on the Great Alfold and Little Alfold, two very fertile plains regions in the country. Manufacturing, including textiles and light equipment, is important. Manufactured products are shipped from this country downriver to the Black Sea, where the manufactured goods are loaded on large ships and exported to other parts of the world.

The city is   a) Budapest   d) Paris   c) London   d) Rome.

It is located in _____.

Government	Transportation	Tourist	Finance	Trade	Manufacturing
___	___	___	___	___	___

g. This largest European city is located on a major river. It is a major port with easy access to the Atlantic Ocean. This large city is the capital of an island nation. In addition to being the capital, it is one of the world's major banking and financial centers. Buckingham Palace and Big Ben are only two of its many tourist attractions.

The city is   a) London   b) Bremen   c) Madrid   d) Belgrade.

It is located in _____.

Government	Transportation	Tourist	Finance	Trade	Manufacturing
___	___	___	___	___	___

Unit 5: More About the Function of Cities

A. Cities Serve a Function (cont.)

2. Cities in Asia

Use **a wall map** or **an atlas** that shows the political and physical features and major cities for countries in Asia. From the description below, identify the city and name the country in which it is located. Also, place a plus sign (+) under the major functions of the city.

a. This city is located on the west coast of a peninsula country. The country in which it is located has the world's second-largest population. It is one of the largest in the country and is the most important port city on the western coast. An important industrial city, steel, textiles, household equipment, and other products are produced here. Oil deposits are found nearby. Like all large cities in this country, it is very crowded. Religious temples associated with the Hindu religion are common. Because the Hindu religion teaches that cows are sacred, it is common to find cows roaming the streets, as they do in other large cities of this country.

The city is   a) Karachi   b) Peking   c) Bombay   d) Rangoon.
It is located in _____.

Government	Transportation	Tourist	Finance	Trade	Manufacturing
_____	_____	_____	_____	_____	_____

b. Located on an island nation, it is the capital and major city. Located near the coast, it is an important transportation center. Since the country has few natural resources, the city must import the materials needed for its very important manufacturing and industrial production. Products manufactured include textiles, steel, ships, and high-tech equipment. Because the country exports the manufactured products to all parts of the world, the city is a trade and transportation center. The country in which this city is located was once part of the large mainland country that is nearby, across the Formosa Strait.

The city is   a) Colombo   b) Singapore   c) Manila   d) Taipei.
It is located in _____.

Government	Transportation	Tourist	Finance	Trade	Manufacturing
_____	_____	_____	_____	_____	_____

Name: _____   Date: _____

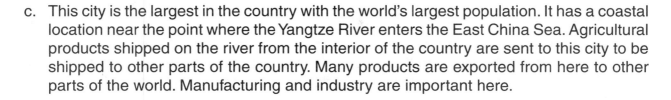

Unit 5: More About the Function of Cities

A. Cities Serve a Function—Cities in Asia (cont.)

c. This city is the largest in the country with the world's largest population. It has a coastal location near the point where the Yangtze River enters the East China Sea. Agricultural products shipped on the river from the interior of the country are sent to this city to be shipped to other parts of the country. Many products are exported from here to other parts of the world. Manufacturing and industry are important here.

The city is   a) Colombo   b) Shanghai   c) Manila   d) Yokohama.

It is located in _____.

Government	Transportation	Tourist	Finance	Trade	Manufacturing
_____	_____	_____	_____	_____	_____

d. This city is located on a small island country that has the same name as the city. It is a major financial and trade center. With its strategic location at the tip of Malaysia, this city has long been an important trading and shipping center. Although lacking natural resources, it is a major manufacturing center, based on imported raw materials. The finished products are then exported to all parts of the world.

The city is   a) Calcutta   b) Tokyo   c) Karachi   d) Singapore.

It is located in _____.

Government	Transportation	Tourist	Finance	Trade	Manufacturing
_____	_____	_____	_____	_____	_____

e. This city is located on the main island of Honshu in one of the world's most prosperous island nations. As the world's largest city located on an island country, it is very crowded. It is the capital and major manufacturing and financial center in this crowded island country. The manufacturing industry is dependent upon imported raw materials, which are then processed into products that are exported all over the world.

The city is a) Calcutta   b) Tokyo   c) Karachi
                    d) Singapore.

It is located in _____.

Government	Transportation	Tourist	Finance	Trade	Manufacturing
_____	_____	_____	_____	_____	_____

Name: _____   Date: _____

Unit 5: More About the Function of Cities

A. Cities Serve a Function (cont.)

3. **Cities in Africa**

Use **a wall map** or **an atlas** that shows the political and physical features and major cities for countries in Africa. From the description below, identify the city and name the country in which it is located. Also, place a plus sign (+) under the major functions of the city.

a. Located near the equator, it is a major city in the country. It is the capital and the main commercial, financial, transportation, and industrial center in the country. Because it is located inland at a higher elevation, the climate is much milder than one would expect for a location so near the equator. The snow-capped peak of Mt. Kilimanjaro is visible from this city.

The city is   a) Dar es Salaam   b) Nairobi   c) Cairo   d) Harate.

It is located in _____.

Government	Transportation	Tourist	Finance	Trade	Manufacturing
_____	_____	_____	_____	_____	_____

b. The largest city in the southernmost country in Africa, its development was based on the mining industry. Without the discovery of minerals, it would not have become the largest city in the country. Diamonds and iron ore are only two of the minerals found near this city. Because of iron, coal, and other minerals nearby, it has become one of the country's most important industrial cities and manufacturing centers.

The city is   a) Nairobi   b) Johannesburg   c) Dar es Salaam   d) Alexandria.

It is located in _____.

Government	Transportation	Tourist	Finance	Trade	Manufacturing	Mining
_____	_____	_____	_____	_____	_____	_____

c. This capital city is located in a landlocked country on the southern fringe of the Sahara Desert. In a country where many people are nomadic, it is its most important city. In addition to its function as a government center, its other main function is as a trade center for local people who regularly bring produce to market. However, it is also a trade center between the countries on the northern coast of Africa and the countries of western Africa. The function of this city is much like the capitals of neighboring countries Burkina Faso, Niger, and Mauritania.

The city is   a) Nairobi   b) Johannesburg   c) Dar es Salaam   d) Bamako.

It is located in _____.

Government	Transportation	Tourist	Finance	Trade	Manufacturing
_____	_____	_____	_____	_____	_____

Name: _____ Date: _____

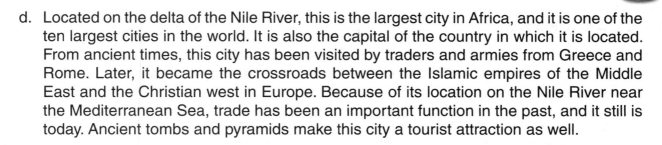

Unit 5: More About the Function of Cities

A. Cities Serve a Function—Cities in Africa (cont.)

d. Located on the delta of the Nile River, this is the largest city in Africa, and it is one of the ten largest cities in the world. It is also the capital of the country in which it is located. From ancient times, this city has been visited by traders and armies from Greece and Rome. Later, it became the crossroads between the Islamic empires of the Middle East and the Christian west in Europe. Because of its location on the Nile River near the Mediterranean Sea, trade has been an important function in the past, and it still is today. Ancient tombs and pyramids make this city a tourist attraction as well.

   The city is   a) Casablanca   b) Tunis   c) Cairo   d) Luanda.

   It is located in _____.

   Government   Transportation   Tourist   Finance   Trade   Manufacturing

   _____   _____   _____   _____   _____   _____

e. This city on the coast near the Gulf of Guinea is located in the African country with the largest population. It is the largest city, but it is not the capital of the country. One of its main functions is as a port city for the oil-rich country in which it is located. Like many of the cities in Africa south of the Sahara, it is a trading center where local citizens market their farm products, as well as clothing and jewelry. Plantation crops that are sold to other countries of the world are shipped from this port.

   The city is   a) Dar es Salaam   b) Monrovia   c) Lagos   d) Cape Town.

   It is located in _____.

   Government   Transportation   Tourist   Finance   Trade   Manufacturing

   _____   _____   _____   _____   _____   _____

f. Located near the Cape of Good Hope, this city is the legislative capital of the country, and it is a financial center. Unlike other countries south of the Sahara, this city is located in a developing country. It is an important port city to which the industrial and manu-factured goods of the country are shipped. Because the climate is mild throughout the year, it is a noted tourist center. From the ports of this city, fruits and vegetables are exported to other countries of the world.

   The city is   a) Cape Town   b) Johannesburg   c) Lagos   b) Mombassa.

   It is located in _____.

   Government   Transportation   Tourist   Finance   Trade   Manufacturing

   _____   _____   _____   _____   _____   _____

Unit 5: More About the Function of Cities

A. Cities Serve a Function (cont.)

4. Cities in Australia

Use **a wall map** or **an atlas** that shows the political and physical features and major cities for Australia. From the description below, identify the city. Also, place a plus sign (+) under the major functions of the city.

a. This city is located in the far southwestern part of the country, in a region with a Mediterranean climate. Inland from this port city is the large, dry interior of the country where cattle and sheep are raised on large ranches. The city is primarily a trading center from which the agricultural products that include wheat, cattle, and sheep are exported. Mining has become more important with the discovery of oil and iron, which are exported from this city. This city is the capital of its province.

The city is   a) Melbourne   b) Adelaide   c) Perth   d) Brisbane.

Government   Transportation   Tourist   Finance   Trade   Manufacturing   Mining

_____   _____   _____   _____   _____   _____   _____

b. Located in the southeastern part of the country, this city is a manufacturing and financial center. It is an important port city, exporting agricultural products for which the country is noted. This city has become a major tourist center. People from all parts of the world come here to visit and enjoy the many water-related events and beautiful buildings. It is the capital of its province, Victoria.

The city is   a) Melbourne   b) Adelaide   c) Perth   d) Brisbane.

Government   Transportation   Tourist   Finance   Trade   Manufacturing   Mining

_____   _____   _____   _____   _____   _____   _____

Name: _____ Date: _____

Unit 6: Using Latitude and Longitude in the Eastern Hemisphere

A. Using Latitude and Longitude

Places on the earth are located using latitude and longitude. Specific locations using latitude and longitude are possible because a grid system is used. Use **Diagram 2** to complete the following exercise to learn how latitude and longitude are used to determine location. You will need blue and red pens or colored pencils.

DIAGRAM 2

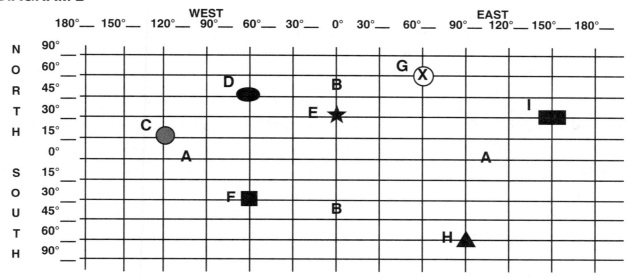

Latitude is measured north and south from the equator. Zero degrees latitude is also known as the **equator**. Latitude locations are always 0 to 90 degrees north or 0 to 90 degrees south. Latitude lines run from east to west, but they measure distance north or south from the equator (0 degrees).

Zero degrees longitude is also known as the **Prime Meridian**. Longitude locations are always 0 to 180 degrees east or 0 to 180 degrees west. **Longitude** lines run north and south, but they measure distance east or west from the Prime Meridian (0 degrees).

1. Fill in the blank by the numbers on **Diagram 2**. On each blank, place the letter E (east), W (west), N (north), S (south).

2. Find "A" on the chart, and then write "equator" on the line. Trace over the equator in blue pen or pencil.

3. The equator is   a) 0   b) 50   c) 30   degrees latitude.

4. Latitude is measured   a) east and west   b) north and south   from the equator.

5. Latitude lines run   a) east and west   b) north and south   but measure distance
   c) east and west   d) north and south.

6. Find "B" on the chart, and then write "Prime Meridian" on the line. Trace over the Prime Meridian in red pen or pencil.

Name: _____   Date: _____

Unit 6: Using Latitude and Longitude in the Eastern Hemisphere

A. Using Latitude and Longitude (cont.)

7. The Prime Meridian is   a) 10   b) 50   c) 0   degrees longitude.

8. Longitude is measured   a) east and west   b) north and south   from the Prime Meridian.

9. Longitude lines run   a) east and west   b) north and south   but measure distance
   c) east and west   d) north and south.

Use **Diagram 2**. On the first blank, write the number and direction for the latitude location. On the second blank, write the number and direction for the longitude location.

10. The location of symbol "C" is _____° _____ latitude and _____° _____ longitude.
11. The location of symbol "D" is _____° _____ latitude and _____° _____ longitude.
12. The location of symbol "E" is _____° _____ latitude and _____° _____ longitude.
13. The location of symbol "F" is _____° _____ latitude and _____° _____ longitude.
14. The location of symbol "G" is _____° _____ latitude and _____° _____ longitude.
15. The location of symbol "H" is _____° _____ latitude and _____° _____ longitude.
16. The location of symbol "I" is _____° _____ latitude and _____° _____ longitude.

The Taj Mahal is one of the most well-known landmarks of the Eastern Hemisphere.

Name: _____ Date: _____

Unit 6: Using Latitude and Longitude in the Eastern Hemisphere

A. Using Latitude and Longitude (cont.)

Use **Map 16** and **an atlas** to complete the following. Circle the letter of the correct location.

1. A location that is 60 degrees north and 30 degrees east is in   a) Finland
   b) the north Atlantic Ocean   c) the Pacific Ocean   d) Australia.

2. A location that is 15 degrees south and 60 degrees east is in   a) the Pacific Ocean
   b) the Mediterranean Sea   c) South Africa   d) the Indian Ocean.

3. A location that is 30 degrees north and 105 degrees east is in   a) Poland   b) China
   c) the Pacific Ocean   d) Democratic Republic of the Congo.

4. A location that is 30 degrees south and 135 degrees east is in   a) Iraq   b) Afghanistan
   c) Australia   d) Saudi Arabia.

5. A location that is 15 degrees north and 105 degrees east is in   a) Cambodia   b) Japan
   c) Indonesia   d) France.

6. A location that is 30 degrees north and 0 degrees longitude is in   a) Germany   b) Russia
   c) Thailand   d) Algeria.

7. A location that is 15 degrees north and 120 degrees east is in   a) India
   b) the Czech Republic   c) the Philippines   d) Japan.

8. A location that is 60 degrees north and 15 degrees east is in   a) Sweden   b) Greenland
   c) England   d) Italy.

9. A location that is 15 degrees north and 0 degrees east is in   a) Ireland   b) Tanzania
   c) Burkina Faso   d) Spain.

10. A location that is 15 degrees north and 75 degrees east is in   a) India   b) Australia
    c) Nepal   d) Pakistan.

11. A latitude location is given as 0 degrees. No longitude is given. The location could be in
    a) Gabon, Congo, Democratic Republic of Congo, Uganda, Somalia, or Indonesia
    b) Gabon, Congo, Dem. Rep. Of Congo, India, Tanzania, the Philippines, or Indonesia
    c) Gabon, Congo, Egypt, India, Tanzania, the Philippines, or Indonesia.

12. A longitude location is given as 75 degrees east. No latitude location is given. The location
    could be in   a) India, Pakistan, China, Kazakhstan, or Russia
    b) India, Pakistan, China, Turkey, or Russia   c) India, Japan, China, Turkey, or Russia.

13. A location between 30 degrees south and 45 degrees south latitude could be in
    a) Algeria, South Africa, or Australia   b) Australia, New Zealand, or South Africa
    c) New Zealand, Australia, or Tanzania.

Name: _____ Date: _____

Unit 6: Using Latitude and Longitude in the Eastern Hemisphere

A. Using Latitude and Longitude (cont.)

MAP 16

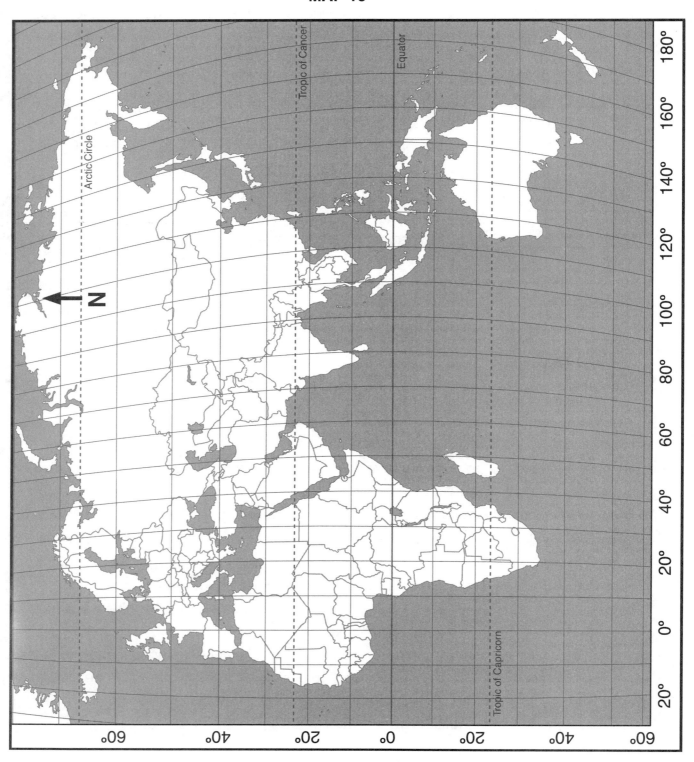

Name: _____   Date: _____

Unit 6: Using Latitude and Longitude in the Eastern Hemisphere

A. Using Latitude and Longitude—Pretest Practice

Complete the blanks using the following terms. A term may be used more than once.

north	south	latitude	longitude	equator	90	180
poles	east	west	zero	Northern	Southern	Eastern
Western	parallel	Prime Meridian				

1. Latitude is measured north and south from the _____.

2. Longitude is measured east and west from the _____.

3. The line of latitude that is zero degrees latitude is the _____.

4. The line of longitude that is zero degrees longitude is the _____.

5. Longitude is measured from zero degrees to _____ degrees.

6. Latitude lines are _____.

7. Longitude lines meet at the _____.

8. The North Pole and South Pole represent _____ degrees latitude.

9. The half of the earth north of the equator is the _____ Hemisphere.

10. The half of the earth south of the equator is the _____ Hemisphere.

11. Any location with a longitude reading east of the Prime Meridian is in the _____ Hemisphere.

12. Any location with a longitude reading west of the Prime Meridian is in the _____ Hemisphere.

13. A location that is 30 degrees north and 45 degrees west is _____ of the Prime Meridian and _____ of the equator.

14. A location that is 30 degrees south and 45 degrees east is _____ of the Prime Meridian and _____ of the equator.

Unit 6: Using Latitude and Longitude in the Eastern Hemisphere

A. Using Latitude and Longitude—Test

1. Latitude is measured north and south from the   a) Prime Meridian   b) equator
   c) International Date Line.

2. Longitude is measured east and west from the   a) Prime Meridian   b) equator
   c) International Date Line.

3. The line of latitude that is zero degrees latitude is the   a) Prime Meridian   b) equator
   c) International Date Line.

4. The line of longitude that is zero degrees longitude is the   a) Prime Meridian   b) equator
   c) International Date Line.

5. Longitude is measured from zero degrees to   a) 60   b) 75   c) 100   d) 180   degrees.

6. Latitude lines   a) run north and south   b) measure distance east and west
   c) are parallel.

7. Longitude lines meet at the   a) equator   b) Prime Meridian   c) Poles
   d) International Date Line.

8. The North Pole and South Pole represent   a) 180   b) 50   c) 90   d) 0   degrees
   latitude.

9. The half of the earth north of the equator is called the   a) Northern   b) Western
   c) Southern   d) Eastern   Hemisphere.

10. The half of the earth south of the equator is called the   a) Northern   b) Western
    c) Southern   d) Eastern   Hemisphere.

11. Any location with a longitude reading east of the Prime Meridian is in the   a) Northern
    Hemisphere b) Western Hemisphere c) Southern Hemisphere d) Eastern Hemisphere.

12. Any location with a longitude reading west of the Prime Meridian is in the   a) Northern
    Hemisphere b) Western Hemisphere c) Southern Hemisphere d) Northern Hemisphere.

13. A location that is 30 degrees north and 45 degrees west is in the   a) Eastern Hemisphere
    b) Western Hemisphere and is north of the   c) equator   d) Prime Meridian.

14. A location that is 30 degrees south and 45 degrees east is in the   a) Eastern Hemisphere
    b) Western Hemisphere and is south of the   c) equator   d) Prime Meridian.

Name: _____   Date: _____

Unit 6: Using Latitude and Longitude in the Eastern Hemisphere

B. Determining the Time for Cities Located at Different Longitudes

The chart below shows the latitude and longitude locations for Cities A, B, C, and D. Across the top of the chart are the longitude readings from 0° to 180° east and west. Along the bottom of the chart are the hourly times at various longitudes, along with the day of the week. The earth rotates 360° on its axis every 24 hours. 360° ÷ 24 hours = 15° per hour. The earth rotates from west to east.

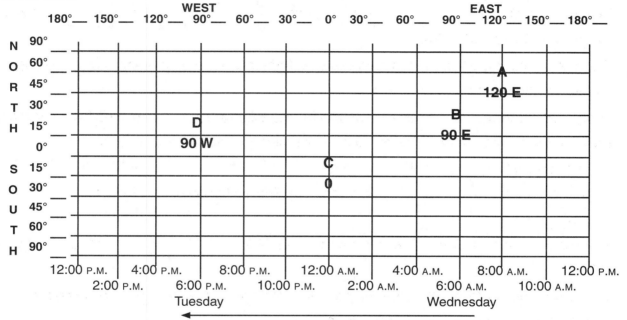

Earth rotates from west to east, so time approaches from the east.

WESTERN HEMISPHERE   EASTERN HEMISPHERE

Refer to the above chart, and then answer the following. Circle the letter of the correct answer.

1. The Prime Meridian is 0° longitude. Trace over the Prime Meridian. Everything from the Prime Meridian west to 180° is the Western Hemisphere. Everything from the Prime Meridian east to 180° is the Eastern Hemisphere.

2. On the chart, it is   a) Wednesday   b) Tuesday   in the Western Hemisphere.

3. On the chart, it is   a) Wednesday   b) Tuesday   in the Eastern Hemisphere.

4. On the chart at 90° west, it is   a) 10:00 P.M. Tuesday   b) 6:00 P.M. Tuesday
    c) 2:00 A.M. Wednesday.

5. On the chart at 90° east, it is   a) 10:00 P.M. Tuesday   b) 6:00 A.M. Wednesday
    c) 2:00 A.M. Wednesday.

Name: _____   Date: _____

Unit 6: Using Latitude and Longitude in the Eastern Hemisphere

B. Determining the Time for Cities Located at Different Longitudes (cont.)

In answering #6, remember that there is a one-hour difference for each 15° of longitude.

6. The time difference between 90° east and 90° west is   a) 6 hours   b) 8 hours
   c) 10 hours   d) 12 hours.

7. The time and day at the Prime Meridian, 0° longitude, is   a) 8:00 A.M. Wednesday
   b) 12:00 A.M. Wednesday   c) 10:00 P.M. Tuesday   d) 2:00 P.M. Wednesday.

8. The time and day at City A is   a) 6:00 A.M. Wednesday   b) 12:00 noon Wednesday
   c) 8:00 A.M. Wednesday.

9. The time and day at City B is   a) 6:00 A.M. Wednesday   b) 10:00 A.M. Wednesday
   c) 2:00 P.M. Wednesday.

10. The time and day at City C is   a) 6:00 A.M. Wednesday   b) 12:00 A.M. Wednesday
    c) 2:00 P.M. Tuesday.

11. The time and day at City D is   a) 12:00 noon Wednesday   b) 6:00 A.M. Wednesday
    c) 6:00 P.M. Tuesday.

12. In City B in two hours, the time and day will be   a) 8:00 A.M. Wednesday
    b) 12:00 noon Wednesday   c) 2:00 P.M. Wednesday.

13. In City C in two hours, the time and day will be   a) 6:00 A.M. Tuesday
    b) 12:00 noon Wednesday   c) 2:00 A.M. Wednesday.

14. In City D in two hours, the time and day will be   a) 8:00 P.M. Tuesday
    b) 12:00 noon Wednesday   c) 8:00 A.M. Wednesday.

Unit 6: Using Latitude and Longitude in the Eastern Hemisphere

B. Determining the Time for Cities Located at Different Longitudes (cont.)

Use **Map 17** to complete the following. Circle the letter of the correct answer.

1. The time and day at the Prime Meridian is 12:00 A.M. Thursday. Trace over the Prime Meridian.
2. The time and day in London, located on the Prime Meridian, is   a) 10:00 P.M. Wednesday   b) 12:00 A.M. Thursday   c) 4:00 A.M. Thursday.
3. The day in the Eastern Hemisphere is   a) Wednesday   b) Thursday.
4. The day in the Western Hemisphere is   a) Wednesday   b) Thursday.

To answer the following questions, assume the time and day at the Prime Meridian is 12:00 A.M. Thursday.

5. The longitude of Shanghai is   a) 90° east   b) 120° east   c) 90° west   d) 0°.
6. The longitude of London is   a) 90° east   b) 120° east   c) 90° west   d) 0°.
7. The time and day in London is   a) 10:00 P.M. Wednesday   b) 12:00 A.M. Thursday   c) 4:00 P.M. Thursday.
8. The number of hours' difference between London and Shanghai is   a) 4   b) 10   c) 8.
9. The time and day in Shanghai is   a) 8:00 A.M. Thursday   b) 2:00 A.M. Friday   c) 6:00 P.M. Wednesday   d) 5:00 A.M. Thursday.
10. The time and day in Bombay is   a) 8:00 A.M. Thursday   b) 10:00 A.M. Thursday   c) 6:00 P.M. Wednesday   d) 5:00 A.M. Thursday.
11. The time and day in Cairo is   a) 8:00 A.M. Thursday   b) 2:00 A.M. Thursday   c) 6:00 P.M. Wednesday   d) 5:00 A.M. Wednesday.
12. The time and day in Dakar is   a) 11:00 P.M. Wednesday   b) 1:00 A.M. Thursday   c) 6:00 P.M. Wednesday   d) 8:00 A.M. Thursday.
13. The time and day in Berlin is about   a) 6:00 A.M. Thursday   b) 8:00 A.M. Thursday   c) 1:00 A.M. Thursday   d) 2:00 A.M. Wednesday.

Assume the time in Canberra, Australia, is 6:00 A.M. Thursday.
14. In one hour, the time and day will be   a) 10:00 A.M. Friday   b) 7:00 A.M. Thursday   c) 1:00 P.M. Thursday   d) 12:00 P.M. Friday.

Assume the time in Bombay, India, is 9:00 P.M. Monday.
15. In two hours, the time and day will be   a) 11:00 A.M. Monday   b) 11:00 P.M. Monday   c) 11:00 A.M. Tuesday   d) 11:00 P.M. Tuesday.

Unit 6: Using Latitude and Longitude in the Eastern Hemisphere

B. Determining the Time for Cities Located at Different Longitudes (cont.)

MAP 17

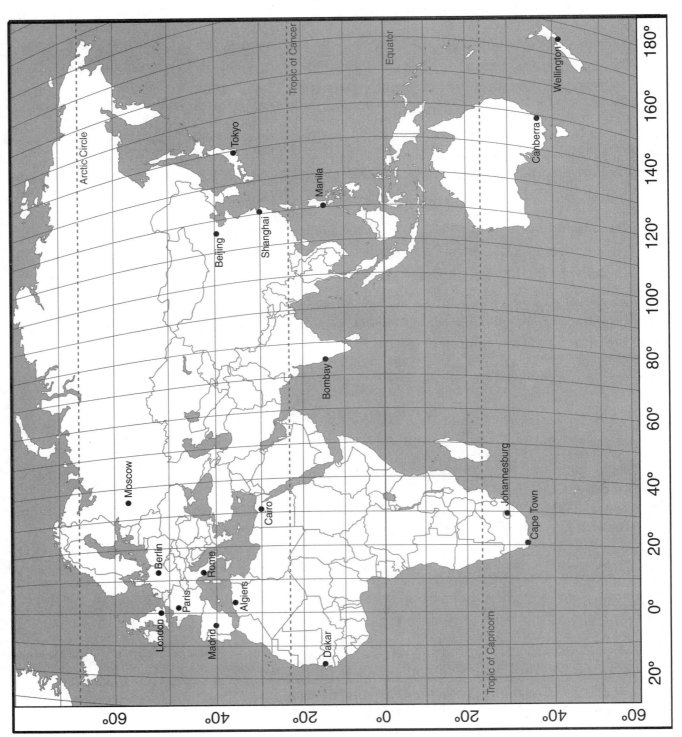

Unit 6: Using Latitude and Longitude in the Eastern Hemisphere

C. Using Latitude and Longitude to Determine Distance Between Locations

When measuring distance in miles using the number of degrees of latitude between two locations, each degree equals approximately 69 miles. This is a constant because the lines of latitude are parallel.

Latitude Chart for Distance
1° of latitude = 69 miles

When measuring distance in miles using the number of degrees of longitude between two locations, the number of miles for each degree will change, based on the latitude of the two locations. The adjustment in miles for each degree of longitude difference is due to the fact that as the lines of longitude approach the Poles, the distance between lines of longitude decreases.

Longitude Chart for Distance
1° of longitude = 69 miles at 0° latitude
1° of longitude = 65 miles at 15° latitude
1° of longitude = 60 miles at 30° latitude
1° of longitude = 35 miles at 60° latitude

To determine the number of miles, 1) determine difference in degrees of latitude or longitude between locations; 2) multiply the difference in degrees of latitude or longitude by 69 miles for latitude. For longitude, use the above chart.

Use **Map 17** to complete the following. Circle the letter of the correct answer.

1. The latitude location of Cairo, Egypt, and Shanghai, China, is   a) 50° north   b) 3° south
   c) 30° north   d) 40° south.
2. The longitude location of Cairo, Egypt, is a) 60° west b) 30° west c) 30° east d) 60° east.
3. The longitude location of Shanghai, China, is   a) 120° west   b) 30° west   c) 120° east
   d) 60° east.
4. The number of degrees longitude difference between Cairo, Egypt, and Shanghai, China,
   is   a) 120°   b) 90°   c) 50°   d) 60°.
5. The distance in miles between Cairo, Egypt, and Shanghai, China, is   a) 90° * 60 miles
   b) 90° * 69 miles   c) 120° * 65 miles   d) 120° * 60 miles.
6. The number of degrees longitude difference between Bombay, India, and Manila, Philippines, is   a) 90°   b) 45°   c) 120°   d) 60°.
7. The distance in miles between Bombay, India, and Manila, Philippines, is   a) 90° * 65
   b) 45° * 65   c) 120° * 65   d) 60° * 65.
8. The number of degrees of latitude difference between Manila, Philippines, and Shanghai,
   China, is   a) 90°   b) 45°   c) 30°   d) 15°.
9. The distance in miles between Manila, Philippines, and Shanghai, China, is   a) 90° * 69
   b) 45° * 65   c) 15° * 69   d) 60° * 65.

Name: _____ Date: _____

Unit 7: Climate in the Eastern Hemisphere

A. Tundra Climate

The **tundra** climate, with long, cold winters and short, warm summers, is found in far northern Europe and Asia. Summers are short and warm with 20 to 24 hours of daylight. Even with the long periods of daylight, only one month has an average monthly temperature above 32°F. The growing season is too short for trees, so the vegetation is made up of mosses and lichens. During the long summer days, the soil will thaw on the surface. However, below the surface, the soil stays permanently frozen. This permanently frozen layer is known as the **permafrost** level. The water from the thawed layer stands on the frozen permafrost, making it very wet and muddy, a place where many insects can survive. The average temperature for the warmest month is 40°F. The average temperature for the coldest month is -20°F. However, in Siberia, the temperatures at some locations become extremely cold during the winter months.

Precipitation falls mainly as snow. While very little snow actually falls, the constantly blowing winds pick up the dry snow and give the impression that greater amounts of snow are falling.

Use **Map 18** and **an atlas** to complete the following.

1. The region with the number 1s is a tundra climate. Color this region black.

2. Place a plus (+) on the blank if the tundra climate is found in the country.
   ___ Spain   ___ Norway   ___ Denmark   ___ Russia   ___ Finland
   ___ Sweden   ___ France

3. A dot on the map locates a city with a tundra climate. Place a plus (+) on the blank that names the city.
   ___ Paris   ___ Moscow   ___ Oslo   ___ Murmansk   ___ Berlin

4. The tundra climate is found on the continents   a) Europe and Africa
   b) Asia and Australia   c) Europe and Asia   d) Africa and Australia.

B. Subarctic (Taiga) Climate

The **subarctic** climate, often called the **taiga**, is found in Europe and Asia. Like the tundra, winters are long and very cold. Because this climate region is located at a high altitude and inland away from large bodies of water, the summer and winter temperatures are influenced

by the large landmass on which it is found. Summers are short, with a growing season of 30 to 60 days. In only one or two months does the average daily temperature rise above 50°F. Snowfall is abundant, and it remains on the ground for over half the year. This climate is known for large forests of coniferous trees that include pines, firs, and spruces. The forests are often referred to as **boreal forests**. The lumber industry is very important in this climate region.

Name: _____ Date: _____

Unit 7: Climate in the Eastern Hemisphere

B. Subarctic (Taiga) Climate (cont.)

Use **Map 18** and **an atlas** to complete the following.

1. The region with the number 2s has a subarctic climate. Color this region purple.
2. Place a plus (+) on the blank if the subarctic climate is found in the country.
   ___ England ___ Finland   ___ Italy   ___Sweden   ___ Norway
   ___ Russia   ___ Australia
3. The subarctic climate has large forests of   a) oak, elm, and maple
   b) fir, pine, and spruce.
4. In the subarctic climate, the growing season is   a) 90 to 120 days   b) 60 to 90 days
   c) 30 to 60 days.

C. Humid Continental Climate

The **humid continental** climate, which has cool summers, is found in much of Europe. Originally, in the humid continental climate, there were many broadleaf trees like maple, oak, birch, and poplar. However, in many regions of Europe, the original forests have been cleared to allow the land to be farmed. The humid continental climate has definite winter and summer seasons. Winters can be mild to very cold, and summers may be warm to hot. Precipitation as rain or snow falls throughout the year. The growing season in the humid continental climate is six months or more. Farming, including grain crops like corn, wheat, and oats, is very important.

Use **Map 18** and **an atlas** to complete the following.

1. The region with the number 3s has a humid continental climate. Color this region blue.
2. Place a plus (+) on the blank if a region of humid continental climate is found in the country.
   ___ England ___ Norway   ___ Poland   ___ Sweden   ___ Ukraine
   ___ Czech Republic   ___ Greece   ___ France   ___ Russia
3. In the humid continental climate,
   a) precipitation seldom falls in summer
   b) precipitation falls mostly in winter
   c) precipitation falls in summer and winter.
4. In the humid continental climate, the growing season is   a) 90 to 120 days
   b) 60 to 90 days   c) 180 to 200 days.

Unit 7: Climate in the Eastern Hemisphere

D. West Coast Marine Climate

In the Northern Hemisphere, the **west coast marine** climate is found on the western coasts of continents between 40° and 60° latitude. In the Southern Hemisphere, the west coast marine climate is actually found on the east coast of continents. Cool summers and mild, wet winters are characteristic. Many days are cloudy, with rain and fog. Rainfall can be as much as 50 to 60 inches per year. The rainfall comes throughout the year. A combination of offshore ocean currents and westerly winds blowing onshore are important factors in explaining why this mild climate is found at such a high latitude.

The west coast marine climate is found along the western coast of Europe, north of 40° north latitude. Here, the westerly winds blow onshore across the North Atlantic ocean current. As the westerly airmasses move onshore, rain and fog are common.

Use **Map 18** and **an atlas** to complete the following.

1. The region with the number 4s has a west coast marine climate. Color this region light green.
2. The west coast marine climate   a) has dry, hot summers and long, cold winters
    b) has cool, wet summers and mild, wet winters.
3. The west coast marine climate is usually found a) on the east coast of continents between 40° and 60° latitude   b) on the west coast of continents between 40° and 60° latitude.
4. Place a plus (+) on the blank if the west coast marine climate is found in the country.
    ____ England ____ Norway   ____ Sweden ____ Ukraine   ____ Slovakia
    ____ Ireland   ____ Denmark ____ New Zealand   ____ Australia ____ South Africa
5. The largest region of west coast marine climate is found in   a) Australia   b) Asia
    c) Europe   d) Africa.

E. Mediterranean Climate

Along the west coast of most continents, a very mild climate called **Mediterranean** is found. This climate is found between 30° and 40° latitude. In Europe, the Mediterranean climate is found near the coastal areas around the Mediterranean Sea. In Africa, a small region of the climate is found at the southern tip of the continent. In Australia, this climate type is found in regions along the southwestern coast. Where the Mediterranean climate is found, summers are hot and dry. The rainfall comes in the winter, which is usually very mild. In summer, skies are usually very clear, with few clouds, if any. The daytime temperatures can become very high. However, nights can be rather cool, as the clear sky allows the earth to lose heat rapidly. The winter temperatures are very mild and sunny. However, most of the rainfall does come in the winter months. The vegetation in the Mediterranean climate consists of shrubs, bushes, and small trees. Grasses grow in clumps and small patches. The Mediterranean climate is a very important agricultural region. Many crops like wheat, fruits, vegetables, olives, and nuts are grown in this climate.

Unit 7: Climate in the Eastern Hemisphere

E. Mediterranean Climate (cont.)

Use **Map 18** and **an atlas** to complete the following.

1. The region with the number 5s has a Mediterranean climate. Color this region dark green.
2. In the Mediterranean climate   a) summers are hot and dry, but winters are mild and wet
   b) summers are cool and wet, but winters are cool and dry.
3. The Mediterranean climate is usually on the   a) east coast   b) west coast   of a continent.
4. Place a plus (+) on the blank if a region of Mediterranean climate is found in the country.
   ____ Spain   ____ Morocco ____ Italy   ____ Poland   ____ China
   ____ Greece   ____ Israel   ____ Turkey   ____ Australia   ____ Algeria
5. The largest region of Mediterranean climate is found in   a) Australia   b) Asia   c) Europe
   d) Africa.

F. Steppe or Semiarid Climate

Where the steppe or semiarid climate is found, the rainfall is 10 to 20 inches per year. This climate type is found in Africa, Asia, and Australia. In steppe regions where the rainfall is nearly 20 inches per year, the vegetation is made up of tall grass. However, in steppe areas where the rainfall is ten inches or less, short, sparse grasses become common. Since the steppe or semiarid regions are often located inland away from large bodies of water, the summer days can become very warm, with temperatures reaching 100°F. Although winters are cooler, the temperatures are still very warm. Because there are few clouds, the night temperatures are much cooler than those during the day. Since the main vegetation is made up of grasses, many people make a living herding sheep and goats in this climate. In Africa, Asia, and Australia, the steppe climate borders large deserts. The closer the steppe climatic region comes to desert regions, the less the rainfall amounts, and the more sparse the grasses.

Use **Map 18** and **an atlas** to complete the following.

1. The region with the number 6s has a steppe climate. Color this region yellow.
2. In the steppe climate, the vegetation is mostly   a) coniferous trees
   b) tall and short grasses   c) trees and tall grass.
3. T/F   In the steppe climate, the herding of goats and sheep is very important.
4. Place a plus (+) on the blank if a region of steppe climate is found in the country.
   ____ China   ____ Australia   ____ Germany   ____ Iraq   ____ Iran
   ____ Jordan   ____ Syria   ____ Angola   ____ Mali   ____ Pakistan
   ____ France   ____ Morocco   ____ Indonesia
5. T/F   Temperatures during the day are much cooler than those at night.

Unit 7: Climate in the Eastern Hemisphere

G. Desert Climate

Desert climates are found in Africa, Asia, and Australia. The desert climate has very hot summers. Winters are mild and warm. Rainfall is less than ten inches per year, and vegetation is very sparse. In places where there is enough grass, nomadic people raise sheep and goats.

Use **Map 18** and **an atlas** to complete the following.

1. The regions with the number 7s have a desert climate. Color these regions brown.

2. Place a plus (+) on the blank if a desert climate is found in some part of the country.

____ Saudi Arabia   ____ Australia ____ France   ____ England ____ Iran

____ Pakistan   ____ Angola   ____ Indonesia ____ Malaysia ____ Niger

____ China   ____ Chad   ____ Libya   ____ Algeria ____ Sudan

____ Burkina Faso

3. Place a plus (+) on the blank if the climate of the country is mostly desert.

____ Dem. Rep. Congo ____ Saudi Arabia ____ Libya   ____ Egypt   ____ India

____ Niger   ____ Mali   ____ Iraq   ____ Uzbekistan

H. Tropical Rain Forest Climate

The **tropical rain forest** climate is found in the tropics in Africa and Asia. In regions where the climate is found, tall trees form a canopy over the ground below. The average monthly temperature is in the high 70s to low 80s. The daytime temperatures are usually in the 90s, with nighttime temperatures in the 70s. In the afternoon, temperatures rise, and as the warm air near the earth's surface begins to rise, thunderstorms develop, bringing heavy downpours of rain.

Use **Map 18** and **an atlas** to complete the following.

1. The regions with the number 8s have a tropical rain forest climate. Color these regions red.

2. Place a plus (+) on the blank if the tropical rain forest climate is found in some part of the country.

____ Gabon   ____ Australia   ____ Dem. Rep. of Congo   ____ England ____ Congo

____ Pakistan ____ Angola   ____ Indonesia   ____ Malaysia

3. The countries located on the equator having a tropical rain forest climate are

   a) Iraq, Algeria, and Indonesia   b) Malaysia, Indonesia, and Dem. Rep. Of Congo

   c) India, China, and Australia   d) the Philippines, Malaysia, and Japan.

4. Countries on the equator having a tropical rain forest climate are located on the continents

   of   a) Africa and Europe   b) Australia and Europe   c) Europe and Asia

   d) Africa and Asia.

Name: _____ Date: _____

Unit 7: Climate in the Eastern Hemisphere

I. Tropical Savanna (Wet and Dry) Climate

The **tropical savanna** climate is found in the tropics of Africa, Australia, and Asia. The tropical savanna has a definite wet season, followed by a very dry season. The wet season comes during the summer; the dry season comes during the winter. Although the seasons are spoken of as summer and winter, the tropical savanna is located so close to the equator that temperatures remain warm throughout the year. During the wet season, rain falls most afternoons and is usually heavy. Lakes are full, and rivers are overflowing. During the dry season, the rains stop, and the lakes and rivers become dry. The vegetation in the savanna climate is made up of mostly tall grasses. However, near the boundary with the tropical rain forest, there are many trees and tall grasses.

Use **Map 18** and **an atlas** to complete the following.

1. The regions with the number 9s have a tropical savanna climate. Color these regions pink.

2. Place a plus (+) on the blank if the tropical savanna climate is found in some part of the country.

   ____ Poland   ____ Italy   ____ Australia ____ Chad   ____ India   ____ Vietnam
   ____ Dem. Rep. Congo   ____ Angola   ____ Russia   ____ Thailand   ____ Cambodia

3. T/F   The tropical savanna climate is found only in countries located in the tropics.

4. T/F   The tropical savanna climate does not have a dry season.

J. Humid Subtropical Climate

In the **humid subtropical** climate, the average summer temperature is often 80°F or more. Winters are cool and moist, with many months having an average temperature of 50°F. The range between the average temperature for the warmest and coolest months is often around 25°. The growing season is 180 to 220 days, making it possible to grow many crops. The humid subtropical climate is found on the southeast coast of most continents, where a warm ocean current flows from the equator toward the north. The winds blow across the warm ocean current, picking up moisture. When the winds reach the mainland, the moisture is dropped as rainfall.

The humid subtropical climate is found along the east coast of China, the islands of Japan, South Korea, and the east coast of Australia.

Use **Map 18** and **an atlas** to complete the following.

1. The regions with the number 10s have a humid subtropical climate. Color these regions orange.

2. Place a plus (+) on the blank if the humid subtropical climate is found in some part of the country.

   ____ India   ____ Thailand ____ Malaysia ____ Indonesia   ____ Japan
   ____ China   ____ Iraq   ____ Australia ____ South Korea

Name: _____   Date: _____

Unit 7: Climate in the Eastern Hemisphere

J. Humid Subtropical Climate (cont.)

3. T/F   The humid subtropical climate is found on the southeast coast of most continents.

4. T/F   The humid subtropical climate is a result of the warm ocean current and onshore winds.

K. Highland Climate

The highland climate is marked by much cooler temperatures than surrounding lower elevations at the same latitude. For each 1,000 feet of elevation, the temperature becomes 3.3 degrees cooler. At higher elevations, the temperature becomes cooler, and the vegetation changes, just as it does if one travels from regions near the equator toward the polar regions. Also, the crops that are grown change as one goes from a lower elevation to one that is higher. Highland climates vary a great deal from place to place. A high plateau surrounded by mountains will have a much milder climate than one found on the exposed ridges of the high mountains at the same elevation. In some highland locations, the temperature and rainfall or snowfall amounts may be very different than at other locations.

Use **Map 18** and **an atlas** to complete the following.

1. The regions with the number 11s have a highland climate. Color these regions gray.

2. Place a plus (+) on the blank if the climate is found in some part of the country.
    ____ Nepal   ____ Australia ____ China   ____ Switzerland   ____ Algeria
    ____ Saudi Arabia

3. The temperature of location "A" at the base of the Himalayan Mountains in India is 80°F. The elevation of the location "A" is 1,000 feet above sea level. Higher in the Himalayas is location "B," which is 10,000 feet above sea level. Assume that the temperature becomes 3.3 degrees cooler for each 1,000 feet of elevation.
    Location "B" is   a) 1,000   b) 9,000   c) 3,000   d) 5,000   feet higher than location "A".

4. The temperature of location "B" will be approximately   a) 40°   b) 60°   c) 30°   d) 10° cooler than at location "A."

5. The temperature at location "B" will be   a) 50°F   b) 60°F   c) 30°F   d) 10°F.

Unit 7: Climate in the Eastern Hemisphere

MAP 18

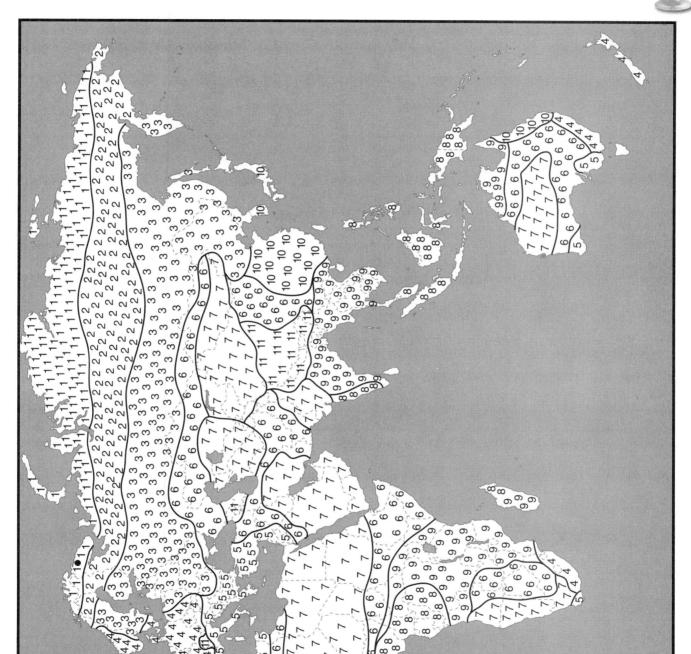

Name: _____ Date: _____

Unit 7: Climate in the Eastern Hemisphere

L. Identifying Climates

For each city listed below, name the climate, the country, and the continent on which the city is located. Find each of the following cities in **an atlas** to identify the corresponding climate region on **Map 18**.

City	Climate	Country	Continent
1. London	_____	_____	_____
2. Cape Town	_____	_____	_____
3. Bombay	_____	_____	_____
4. Moscow	_____	_____	_____
5. Canberra	_____	_____	_____

6. Name some types of clothing you would pack for a trip to London.

_____

_____

7. Name some types of clothing you would pack for a trip to Moscow during the winter.

_____

_____

8. Name some types of clothing you would pack for a trip to Bombay.

_____

_____

9. Name some types of clothing you would pack for a trip to Canberra during the summer.

_____

_____

10. Name some types of clothing you would pack for a trip to Cape Town during the winter.

_____

_____

Name: _____ Date: _____

Unit 7: Climate in the Eastern Hemisphere

L. Identifying Climates (cont.)

Using **Map 18** and **an atlas**, place a plus (+) under the continent if the climate is found on the continent.

	Africa	Australia	Asia	Europe
1. Tundra	_____	_____	_____	_____
2. Tropical Rain Forest	_____	_____	_____	_____
3. West Coast Marine	_____	_____	_____	_____
4. Mediterranean	_____	_____	_____	_____
5. Humid Continental	_____	_____	_____	_____
6. Subarctic (Taiga)	_____	_____	_____	_____
7. Steppe (Semiarid)	_____	_____	_____	_____
8. Desert	_____	_____	_____	_____
9. Highland	_____	_____	_____	_____
10. Tropical Savanna	_____	_____	_____	_____
11. Humid Subtropical	_____	_____	_____	_____

12. Climate types that are found in Europe and Asia but not found in Africa and Australia are

    a) tundra and tropical savanna   b) humid subtropical and steppe

    c) subarctic and tundra   d) Mediterranean and desert.

13. Climate types that are found in Africa and Asia but not found in Europe are the

    a) tropical savanna and Mediterranean   b) tropical rain forest and tropical savanna

    c) tundra and subarctic   d) semiarid and desert.

Name: _____   Date: _____

Unit 7: Climate in the Eastern Hemisphere

L. Identifying Climates—Pretest Practice

Use the terms below to complete the blanks. Write the correct answer in each blank.

**desert   3.3   humid subtropical   highland   tropical rain forest   Mediterranean
west coast marine   tundra   China   North Atlantic**

1. The type of climate found in the high Himalayan Mountains is _____.

2. The humid subtropical climate is found along the east coast of _____.

3. The climate type found on the east coast of Australia is _____.

4. The climate type found on the southwest coast of Europe and the northwest coast of Africa between 30° and 40° north latitude is _____.

5. The climate type found in the Democratic Republic of Congo near the Congo River is

    _____.

6. The climate type found on the west coast of Europe at latitudes above 40° north is

    _____.

7. Most of Saudi Arabia has the _____ climate.

8. The _____ climate is found in the northernmost parts of Europe and

    Asia.

9. The tropical savanna climate is found on the northern and southern borders of the

    _____ climate.

10. The climate noted for hot, dry summers and mild, wet winters, located between 30° and 40°

    north latitude around the Mediterranean Sea is the _____ climate.

11. When climbing up a mountain, for each 1,000 feet of eleva-

    tion, the temperature will become _____

    degrees cooler.

12. The climate type found in Malaysia, Indonesia, and the

    Philippines is the _____.

Name: _____ Date: _____

Unit 7: Climate in the Eastern Hemisphere

L. Identifying Climates—Test

Circle the letter of the correct answer.

1. The type of climate found in the high Himalayan Mountains is   a) highland
   b) west coast marine   c) tundra   d) humid subtropical.

2. In the Eastern Hemisphere, the type of climate found in far northern Europe and Asia is
   a) highland   b) west coast marine   c) tundra   d) humid subtropical.

3. The climate type found on the southeast coast of China is   a) Mediterranean
   b) humid continental   c) tundra   d) humid subtropical.

4. The climate type found around the Mediterranean Sea between 30° and 40° north latitude is
   a) Mediterranean   b) humid continental   c) tundra   d) humid subtropical.

5. The climate type found near the Congo River in Africa is   a) tropical savanna
   b) tropical rain forest   c) subarctic   d) west coast marine.

6. The climate type found on the west coast of Europe at latitudes between 40° and 60° north is
   a) Mediterranean   b) west coast marine   c) steppe   d) desert.

7. Most of Saudi Arabia has the   a) desert   b) west coast marine   c) tropical rain forest
   d) tundra   climate.

8. The tropical savanna climate is found on the north and south borders of the
   a) Mediterranean   b) humid subtropical   c) steppe   d) tropical rain forest   climate.

9. When climbing higher up a mountain, for each 1,000 feet of elevation, the temperature will
   become approximately   a) 3.3°   b) 8°   c) 1°   d) 10°   cooler.

10. In Europe, Asia, and Australia, the climate bordering the desert is most often the
    a) Mediterranean   b) west coast marine   c) steppe or semiarid   d) humid subtropical.

Name: _____　Date: _____

Unit 8: Understanding Developed and Underdeveloped Countries

Information about a country typically includes the area, the number of people, the climate, the largest cities, and the natural resources found there. It is also important to know how people make a living, how crowded the countries are, the medical services available for the people, the education level, and religious preferences. A very important bit of information relates to the age levels found in a country. Is most of the population young? Is most of the population middle-aged? Are there large numbers of older people in the population?

A. Population Pyramids

Population pyramids show the percentage of people represented by different age groups. From the population pyramid, one can tell if most of the people are younger or if most are older. Knowing which age groups form the largest percentage of the population will help determine how the resources of a country should be used to provide services for the people.

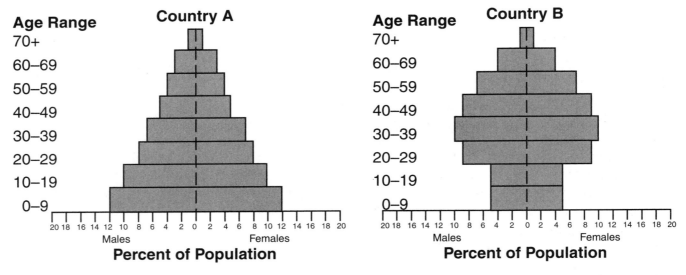

The more a population pyramid is shaped like a Christmas tree, the younger the population. Any other shape of the pyramid must be analyzed to determine the age groups that make up most of the population.

Use Country A to complete the following questions. Assume that Country A has a population of 1,000 people.

1. In Country A, the percent of the total population that is in the age group 0–9 years is
   a) 10%　b) 50%　c) 24%　d) 5%.

2. In Country A, the number of males in the age group 0–9 years is　a) 120　b) 90　c) 60
   d) 10.

3. In Country A, the number of females in the age group 0–9 years is　a) 120　b) 90
   c) 60　d) 10.

4. The total number of males and females in the age group 0–9 is　a) 120　b) 180　c) 240
   d) 100.

Name: _____ Date: _____

Unit 8: Understanding Developed and Underdeveloped Countries

A. Population Pyramids (cont.)

5. In Country A, most of the population is   a) young   b) middle-aged   c) old.

Use Country B to complete the following questions. Assume that Country B has a population of 1,000 people.

1. In Country B, the percent of the population that is in the age group 0–9 years is   a) 10%   b) 50%   c) 30%   d) 5%.

2. In Country B, the number of males in the age group 0–9 years is   a) 50   b) 90   c) 60   d) 100.

3. In Country B, the number of females in the age group 0–9 years is   a) 120   b) 50   c) 60   d) 100.

4. The total number of males and females in the age group 0–9 is   a) 120   b) 180   c) 240   d) 100.

5. In Country B, most of the population is   a) young   b) middle-aged   c) old.

Data from a population pyramid can be used to predict the kind of services the country must provide for its citizens. If the pyramid looks like a Christmas tree, then the country could benefit from spending money on school buildings, education programs, job training, and medical programs to develop the talents of the young. If the pyramid has a shape like a downward-pointing triangle, which shows the majority of the population is older, then the country will need to spend more money on health services and other needs for the older population.

The population pyramids for developed and underdeveloped countries are often very different. The population pyramids below are examples of these pyramids. In the Eastern Hemisphere, a large number of underdeveloped countries are found south of the Sahara Desert in Africa, or what is known as "sub-Saharan Africa." A large number of developed countries are found in Europe.

Underdeveloped countries usually have a large percentage of the population engaged in subsistence agriculture or working on large plantations. Subsistence agriculture is raising crops for family use with little, if any, of the crop sold. The large plantations in underdeveloped countries are usually owned by large companies, and the wages paid to the workers are minimal. In underdeveloped countries, a small percentage of the population is engaged in manufacturing and industry. Many times, the natural resources of the country are exported, rather than used to build manufacturing and industry within the country.

Developed countries usually have a large percentage of the population engaged in manufacturing and industry. A very small percentage of the population is engaged in subsistence agriculture. Those engaged in agriculture raise crops to sell products. This type of agriculture is called commercial agriculture.

Name: _____   Date: _____

Unit 8: Understanding Developed and Underdeveloped Countries

A. Population Pyramids (cont.)

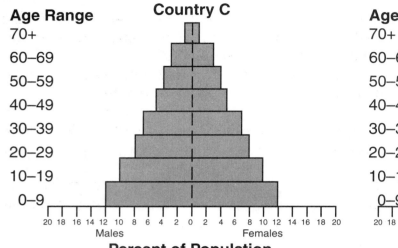

Use the **population pyramid for Country C** to complete the following. Place a plus (+) on the blank by the statement if it is true for Country C.

1. _____ There is a larger number of people in the age range from 0 to 19 than in the age range 60 to 70+.

2. _____ There is a larger number of people in the age range 60 to 70+ than in the age range 0 to 19.

3. _____ The country should be spending more money on services for those who are age 0 to 19, rather than for those who are 60 to 70+.

4. _____ The country should be spending more money on services for those who are 60 to 70+, rather than for those who are ages 0 to 19.

5. _____ The shape of the pyramid shows that there are large numbers of young people who have not yet completed their education to enter the workforce.

Use the **population pyramid for Country D** to complete the following. Place a plus (+) on the blank if it is true for Country D.

6. _____ There is a larger number of people in the age range from 0 to 19 than in the age range 30 to 49.

7. _____ There is a larger number of people in the age range from 30 to 49 than in the age range from 0 to 19.

8. _____ The country should be spending more money on services for those who are 60 to 70+, rather than for those who are ages 0 to 19.

9. _____ The shape of the pyramid shows that there are large numbers of people who should have completed their education and entered the workforce.

Name: _____   Date: _____

Unit 8: Understanding Developed and Underdeveloped Countries

B. Population Density

Knowing the population of a country is important information. However, it is important to know how crowded or densely populated a country is. Are most of the people crowded into selected locations, or are people spread evenly throughout the country?

To determine population density for a country, the total population must be divided by the area. Area of a country may be given in number of square miles or kilometers.

Example: Country A has a population of 1,000. The area is 100 square miles. 1,000 ÷ 100 = 10. The population density is 10 persons per square mile.

A question that must then be asked is: How are the people distributed? Are there actually ten people on each square mile, or are most people located so that some regions of the country are very crowded and other regions are sparsely populated?

Complete the chart below to find the population density for these Eastern Hemisphere countries. Numbers for population and area have been rounded and projected. Note that the area is shown in square kilometers.

	Country	Population		Area (Sq. Km)		Density of Population (Per Sq. Km)
1.	China	1,400,000,000	÷	9,600,000	=	_____
2.	Egypt	79,000,000	÷	1,001,000	=	_____
3.	Pakistan	170,000,000	÷	804,000	=	_____
4.	Japan	127,000,000	÷	378,000	=	_____
5.	Nigeria	160,000,000	÷	924,000	=	_____

Use the above chart to answer the following. Circle the letter of the correct answer.

6. The country with the highest density of population is   a) China   b) Japan   c) Egypt   d) Nigeria.

7. Which country has a lower density of population?   a) Pakistan   b) China

The density of population figures in the above chart tell how many people there are per square kilometer of land area. However, in most of these countries, there are large areas of land that have few people living there, if any. There are also areas of the country where the density of population is much greater than the average for the country.

Name: _____ Date: _____

Unit 8: Understanding Developed and Underdeveloped Countries

B. Population Density (cont.)

Use **Map 19**, **Map 20**, and **an atlas** to complete the following. The countries A. China, B. Egypt, C. Pakistan, D. Japan, E. Nigeria, and F. India are located on Map 19 and Map 20 with the letter preceding the country's name. Connect the dashed line inside each country to locate the areas where the density of population is much greater than the average for the country. Color the regions inside the dashed lines brown.

1. In China, the most densely populated region of the country is   a) the far western region

    b) the far northern region   c) the eastern region   of the country.

2. In Egypt, the most densely populated region of the country is   a) the region near the Nile River   b) the desert region of the west   c) the region near the Red Sea.

3. In Pakistan, the most densely populated region of the country is

    a) the dry western regions of the country   b) the Thar Desert region

    c) the region in and around the Indus River.

4. The best statement describing the density of population in Japan is

    a) Hokkaido, the island in the north is   b) the islands of Honshu, Kyushu, Shikoku are

    c) the island of Honshu is   the most densely populated.

5. In Nigeria, the most densely populated part of the country is

    a) in the south near the Gulf of Guinea   b) in the central part of the country

    c) all regions are equally densely populated.

6. The population figures for a country tell   a) how many people live in the country

    b) where the most densely populated regions are

    c) how many people there are per square kilometer or square mile.

7. The density of population is determined by the formula   a) area ÷ population

    b) population ÷ area   c) area + population.

8. The density of population figure tells   a) how many people live in the country

    b) where the most densely populated regions are

    c) how many people there are per square kilometer or square mile.

9. Once the density of population is known, it is important to know

    a) where the center of the country is

    b) where people are more crowded than the average

    c) where the rivers are located.

Name: _____   Date: _____

Unit 8: Understanding Developed and Underdeveloped Countries

B. Population Density (cont.)

MAP 20

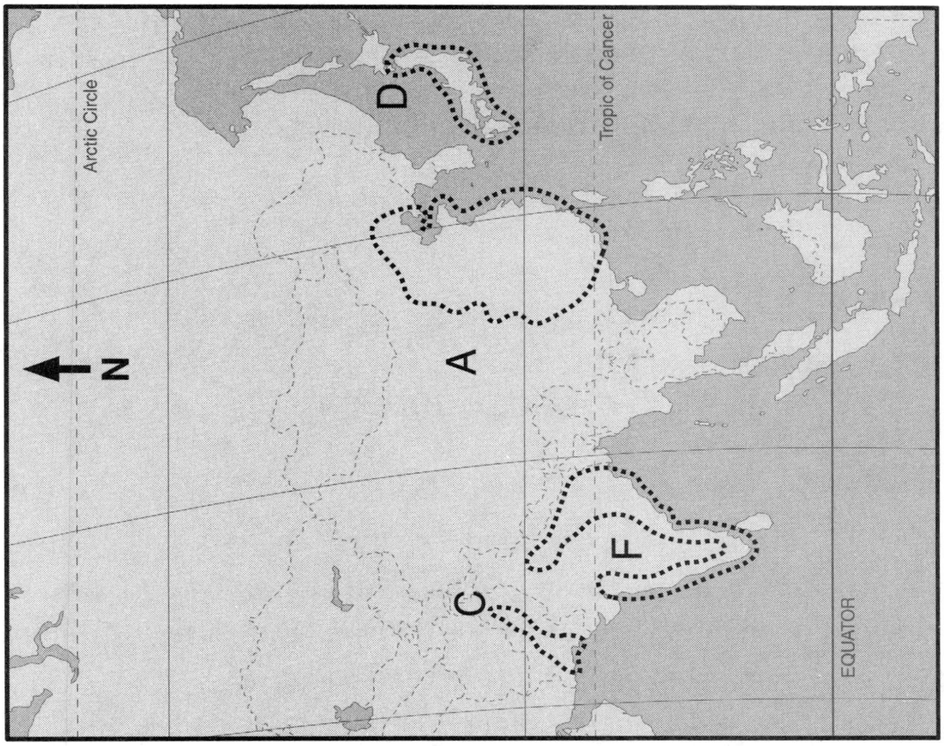

MAP 19

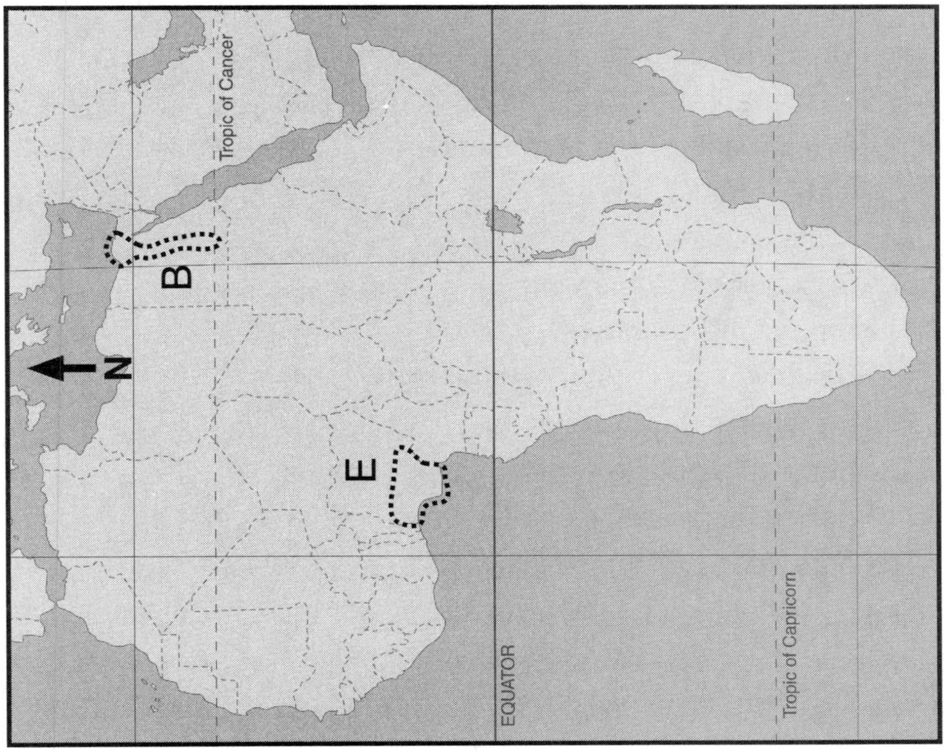

Name: _____   Date: _____

Unit 8: Understanding Developed and Underdeveloped Countries

C. Subsistence Agriculture vs. Manufacturing

Pie Graph A and Pie Graph B below are for two different countries. Each pie graph illustrates the percent of people in each country who live by subsistence agriculture. Remember, subsistence agriculture is when people raise the crops they need to live, with little, if anything, left to be sold for money that might be used for other needs.

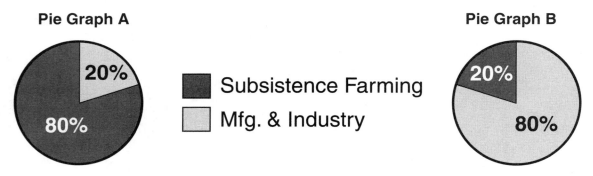

1. It is more likely that an underdeveloped country will have more people engaged in subsistence farming to live. In the above graphs,   a) Graph A   b) Graph B   indicates that more people are engaged in subsistence farming. Therefore,   a) Graph A   b) Graph B is more likely to represent an underdeveloped country.

2. It is more likely that a developed country will have more people engaged in jobs in manufacturing and industry than in subsistence farming. In the above graphs,   a) Graph A   b) Graph B   indicates that more people are engaged in manufacturing and industry. Therefore,   a) Graph A   b) Graph B   is more likely to represent a developed country.

3. Place a + on the blank by the statement, if the statement is important in gaining a clear picture of what a country is like.

_____ The climate of the country.

_____ The population of the country.

_____ The area of the country.

_____ The density of population of the country.

_____ The physical features of the country.

_____ The percent of people in different age groups.

_____ The natural resources the county has.

_____ The percentage of people in subsistence farming.

_____ The percentage of people who make a living in manufacturing and industry.

Name: _____ Date: _____

Unit 8: Understanding Developed and Underdeveloped Countries

D. Gross National Product

Developed and underdeveloped countries differ in ways other than by the comparison of the percentage of people engaged in subsistence agriculture and manufacturing.

The total value of all goods and services produced in a country, known as the **Gross National Product** or **GNP**, the average education level of the people, and life expectancy are other pieces of data that separate underdeveloped from developed countries.

The total Gross National Product (GNP) figure is divided by the population of the country to give a GNP figure on an individual basis. Highly developed countries usually have an average GNP of $20,000 or more. In underdeveloped countries, the average GNP is often $500 or less.

Chart I below shows the eight countries with the highest GNP in the Eastern Hemisphere. Locate each of these countries using an atlas. Place a plus (+) on the blank below the continent on which the country is located.

CHART I

Country	Europe	Asia	Africa	Australia
1. Monaco	_____	_____	_____	_____
2. Liechtenstein	_____	_____	_____	_____
3. Norway	_____	_____	_____	_____
4. Qatar	_____	_____	_____	_____
5. Luxembourg	_____	_____	_____	_____
6. Denmark	_____	_____	_____	_____
7. Sweden	_____	_____	_____	_____
8. Netherlands	_____	_____	_____	_____

Name: _____ Date: _____

Unit 8: Understanding Developed and Underdeveloped Coun-

D. Gross National Product (cont.)

Chart II below shows nine of the lowest GNP countries in the Eastern Hemisphere. Locate each of these countries using an atlas. Place a + mark on the blank below the continent on which the country is located.

CHART II

	Country	Europe	Asia	Africa	Australia
9.	Eritrea	_____	_____	_____	_____
10.	Madagascar	_____	_____	_____	_____
11.	Ethiopia	_____	_____	_____	_____
12.	Niger	_____	_____	_____	_____
13.	Malawi	_____	_____	_____	_____
14.	Sierra Leone	_____	_____	_____	_____
15.	Liberia	_____	_____	_____	_____
16.	Burundi	_____	_____	_____	_____
17.	Dem. Rep. of Congo	_____	_____	_____	_____

Use **Chart I** and **Chart II** to answer the following.

18. The countries with the highest GNP are located in   a) Africa and Europe
    b) Europe and Asia   c) Australia and Asia   d) Africa and Australia.

19. The countries with the lowest GNP are located in   a) Australia   b) Asia
    c) Europe   d) Africa.

20. The African countries with the lowest GNP are located   a) north   b) south   of the Sahara Desert.

Name: _____ Date: _____

Unit 9: Reading Exercises to Determine the Country

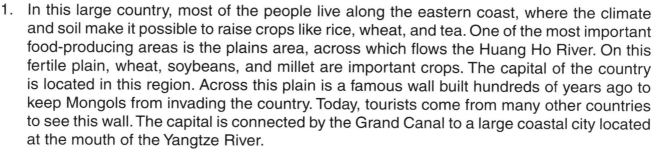

Read each of the following country descriptions. Answer the questions that follow each description.

1. In this large country, most of the people live along the eastern coast, where the climate and soil make it possible to raise crops like rice, wheat, and tea. One of the most important food-producing areas is the plains area, across which flows the Huang Ho River. On this fertile plain, wheat, soybeans, and millet are important crops. The capital of the country is located in this region. Across this plain is a famous wall built hundreds of years ago to keep Mongols from invading the country. Today, tourists come from many other countries to see this wall. The capital is connected by the Grand Canal to a large coastal city located at the mouth of the Yangtze River.

    In the westernmost part of the country, there are high plateaus and mountains. The Takla Makan Desert and Gobi Desert are located in the western region of the country. This country, located in Asia, has the world's largest population. In area, it is the third-largest country in the world. This country is rich in natural resources, including iron, coal, and oil. This country shares a long border with Russia and Mongolia.

    This country is   a) India   b) China   c) Russia   d) Iran.

2. This country, located in the Middle East, is an oil-rich country. Although it is a Middle Eastern country, most people are Persian rather than Arab. The major physical features of the country include the Zagros Mountains near the Persian Gulf, the Elburz Mountains near the Caspian Sea, and a high, dry plateau between the mountain ranges. The capital and major city is located south of the Elburz Mountains in the northern part of the country. The government is controlled by an Islamic theocracy. In their daily lives, people are expected to follow very strict Islamic guidelines relating to dress, music, and prayer.

    The country is   a) Iran   b) India   c) Israel   d) Japan.

3. The Rub' al Khali Desert covers most of this Middle Eastern country. Most people are Arabs, and the Islamic religion is the state religion. Mecca and Medina, the two cities most important to followers of the Islamic religion, are located in this country. Although the country is largely desert, it is wealthy because of the oil deposits found there. Many believe that 25 percent of the world's known oil reserves are located in this country. This country is by far the largest country located on the peninsula surrounded by the Red Sea, Persian Gulf, and Arabian Sea.

    The country is   a) Syria   b) Jordan   c) Saudi Arabia   d) Iraq.

Name: _____ Date: _____

Unit 9: Reading Exercises to Determine the Country

4. With over 6,500,000 square miles, this country is the world's largest country in area. The Ural Mountains divide the European and Asian parts of the country. Although there are huge reserves of oil, iron, coal, and other minerals, the far northern location makes large parts of the country unsuitable for agriculture. Once a powerful communist country made up of 15 republics that included people from many ethnic groups, the country was known as the Union of Soviet Socialist Republics. Today, many of the provinces have gained independence, and the country is known by the name of the largest of the former republics.

   The country is   a) Turkmenistan   b) Russia   c) Iran   d) China.

5. This country is located in the Middle East and is a neighbor of Saudi Arabia. Next to Saudi Arabia, the country has the largest oil reserves in the region. A large part of the country is desert, mountainous, or dry plateau, but the heartland of the country is the historically famous Mesopotamia. Most of the people live in the cities that are located on this fertile plain of Mesopotamia. The Tigris and Euphrates Rivers flow through Mesopotamia and into the Persian Gulf. Kirkuk, Mosul, Baghdad, and the port city Basra are major cities.

   The country is   a) Turkey   b) Iraq   c) Iran   d) Saudi Arabia.

6. Two countries located in West Africa were established as a home for freed slaves from the United States and Great Britain. Today, both countries have the problems of many other underdeveloped countries on the continent of Africa. Most people are very poor and must eke out a living by subsistence farming. Subsistence farming means that the crops raised are used for food for the  family, with very little left to be sold. Subsistence crops include rice and cassava. There are large commercial plantations where coffee and cacao are produced to be sold on the world market. However, these plantations are owned by large companies, and the wages paid are minimal. There are mineral deposits in these two countries that include iron ore and diamonds. But in underdeveloped countries, most minerals are exported, rather than used to develop industry and manufacturing within the country.

   The countries are   a) Namibia and Botswana   b) Tanzania and Kenya
      c) Liberia and Sierra Leone   d) Zimbabwe and Zambia.

Name: _____ Date: _____

Unit 9: Reading Exercises to Determine the Country

7. The Olduvai Gorge is located in this east African country. It is in this gorge that many scientists have found evidence that indicates that the gorge was the home of early man. During the period from the eighth to the twelfth centuries, Arab traders, as well as traders from India, came across the Indian Ocean to the east coast of this country to trade with the native population. Little was known about the interior of the country until explorers from Europe arrived in the nineteenth centuries. The country was a part of the British Empire until 1961, when the country became independent. As in most of the countries south of the Sahara, the majority of the people are engaged in agriculture. Although many depend on subsistence farming to survive, cash crops like coffee, tea, and cotton are produced. Dar es Salaam is a large city located along the coast near the Indian Ocean. Inland away from the coast, the land rises to a higher plateau region with vegetation that is largely grass, with some trees. Along the western border of the country is the long, narrow Great Rift Valley with Lake Tanganyika.

The country is   a) Mozambique   b) Zambia   c) Tanzania   d) Kenya.

8. This west African country has the largest population in Africa. It is one of the world's fastest-growing countries in population and is presently the world's tenth-largest in population. It is a country with many natural resources, including iron ore, coal, natural gas, and oil. Its oil deposits are so great that it is a major oil-exporting country. Along the coast, the climate is tropical, with forests and much rainfall. As one goes north, the rainfall amounts decrease, and the vegetation changes from trees to grass, and finally, to desert. Along the coast, agricultural products include cocoa, palm oil, and rubber produced on large commercial plantations for export. Most people depend on subsistence agriculture, raising crops like cassava, yams, millet, and sorghum. In the northern part of the country, most people are Islamic. In the southern half of the country, many people are Christian. Major cities in the south are Lagos and Ibadan. Kano is a major city in the north.

The country is   a) Ghana   b) Benin   c) Nigeria   d) Niger.

9. This developing country is located on the southern tip of Africa. It has many natural resources and is the world's leading producer of gold and platinum. Most of the natural resources are used to manufacture items such as machinery, automobiles, textiles, and chemicals for export to all parts of the world. In this country, most people are employed in manufacturing and industry. Cape Town and Johannesburg are the major cities.

As Europeans gained control of the country and moved inland, they settled on land that belonged to the natives. War resulted, and the Europeans established a policy called "apartheid," which separated the Europeans and the natives with respect to where people could live, the jobs they could hold, and also involved other restrictions. This led to many years of conflict between the Europeans and the native African population. Today, the policy of "apartheid" has been abolished, and the restrictions according to race have been removed.

The country is   a) South Africa   b) Botswana   c) Gabon   d) Mozambique.

Name: _____   Date: _____

Unit 10: Regions of Conflict

Countries and their neighbors often have issues over which there is disagreement. Within countries, there are often conflicts that occur among the various groups who make up the country. Some conflicts are settled in a friendly manner. Often, however, conflicts result in war, the loss of life, and destruction for the countries involved.

Conflicts occur for many reasons. Conflicts develop when countries cannot agree on boundaries. Religious differences may also cause conflict. The possession of mineral deposits has often caused conflict. In dry regions, conflict over water may occur. Political disagreements over the form of government are also common.

A. Conflict Between Countries

1. North Korea and South Korea

Read the following, and then complete the exercise that follows.

At the end of World War II, conflict began in Korea between those who wanted a communist form of government and those who wanted a democratic form of government. Before the conflict ended, other major countries of the world had been drawn into the conflict. The United States was drawn into the conflict to support those who favored a democracy. China was drawn into the conflict to support those who wanted a communist government. When neither side could defeat the other, the fight that had begun over the type of government the country would have became a conflict over the location of the boundary that would divide the two countries. The conflict ended with the countries divided at 38° north latitude (38th Parallel). The two new countries became North Korea, with a dictator and communist government, and South Korea, with a president and democratic government. The 38th Parallel that divides the countries has remained a potential area of conflict, with both countries having soldiers stationed on each side of the border in an area called the **Demilitarized Zone (DMZ)**.

Use **Map 21** to complete the following. Each of the countries below is located on Map 21 with the letter before the name of the country. Each city is located with a dot on the map.

**a. North Korea   b. South Korea   c. China   d. The United States
e. Seoul   f. Pyongyang**

1. Locate North Korea, and color the country red.
2. Locate South Korea, and color the country blue.
3. Locate China, and color the country brown.
4. Locate the United States, and color the country green.

Name: _____   Date: _____

Unit 10: Regions of Conflict

A. Conflict Between Countries—North and South Korea (cont.)

5. The conflict between North Korea and South Korea began as a conflict over
   a) religion   b) water   c) type of government
   d) the boundary to separate the countries.

6. The conflict over the type of government became a conflict over a) religion   b) water
   c) the boundary that would separate North Korea and South Korea.

7. On Map 21, place the letter "e" by the dot that locates Seoul, the capital of South Korea.

8. On Map 21, place the letter "f" by the dot that locates Pyongyang, the capital of North Korea.

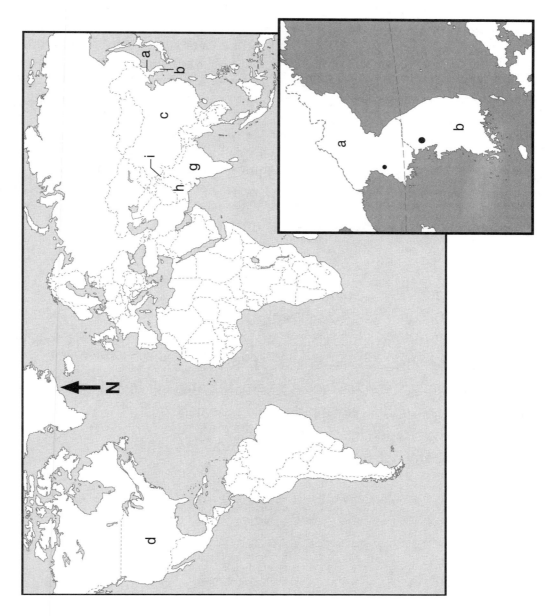

MAP 21

Name: _____   Date: _____

Unit 10: Regions of Conflict

A. Conflict Between Countries (cont.)

2. India and Pakistan

Read the following, and then complete the exercise that follows.

      The countries that today are India and Pakistan were once a part of the British Empire. In 1947, Great Britain divided the region into present-day Pakistan and India. Later, Great Britain granted each country its independence. In granting independence, the British drew the boundary lines that would determine the territory for each country.

      Most of the people of Pakistan were Muslims and belonged to the Islamic religion. In India, most people were Hindu, but there were also a large number of Muslims. Many Muslims chose to move to Pakistan, but others wanted to remain in India. A major disagreement between the two countries arose over a beautiful region known as Kashmir. This fertile valley is located at the base of the Himalayan Mountains. Many Hindus lived in Kashmir, which was ruled by a Hindu prince. However, the majority of the people in Kashmir were Muslims. Pakistan and India each believed that Kashmir should be a part of its country. Today, the disagreement has not been settled, and a number of battles between the armed forces from both countries has been fought over control of the region.

Use **Map 21** and **an atlas** to complete the following. Each of the countries/regions below is indicated on Map 21 by a lowercase letter.

g. India   **h. Pakistan**   **i. Kashmir**

1. Locate Kashmir, and color it blue.
2. Locate India, and color it yellow.
3. Locate Pakistan, and color it brown.
4. The conflict between Pakistan and India began as a political conflict over
    a) whether Kashmir would be Islamic or Hindu.
    b) whether Kashmir would be a part of India or Pakistan.
5. A major factor that prevents resolving the conflict is
    a) religious conflict between Muslims and Hindus   b) water rights
    c) mineral rights.

Name: _____   Date: _____

Unit 10: Regions of Conflict

A. Conflict Between Countries (cont.)

3. Israel and Palestine

Read the following, and then complete the exercise that follows.

The city of Jerusalem has been a source of conflict for Jews, Muslims, and Christians for centuries.

Following World War II, the United Nations established the country of Israel as a Jewish country on the Mediterranean coast. This new country was carved out of a region that was inhabited by Arabs. The Arabs were mostly Muslims who had lived in the region for centuries. To form the new country, it was necessary to move the Arabs to a new location outside the boundary of Israel. Jewish people from all over the world came to the new country. Most came from countries in war-torn Europe, including Russia.

Neighboring Arab countries, where most people are Muslim, have gone to war with Israel on a number of occasions since Israel was established. Sources of conflict result from the fact that when Israel was established, many Palestinians were forced to leave the land. There have been conflicts over the boundary of Israel with surrounding countries, and a conflict over control of the city of Jerusalem. These conflicts have been intensified by the religious animosities that exist between some Jews and Muslims. Part of the conflict over the ancient city of Jerusalem exists because it is a holy city to Christians, Jews, and Muslims.

Following a six-day war with Jordan in 1967, Israel seized the region known as the "West Bank." Large numbers of Jews have gone into the West Bank and developed settlements. These settlements are an additional source of conflict between the Jewish settlers and the Arabs.

Use **Map 22** and **an atlas** to complete the following. Each of the countries, cities, or physical features listed below is indicated on Map 22 by a lowercase letter, or a letter and a symbol.

a. Jordan   **b. Israel**   **c. Egypt**   **d. Lebanon**   **e. Syria**
f. ～～ **Jordan River**   **g.** (⬭) **Negev Desert**   **h.** ⬭ **Sea of Galilee**
i. • Jerusalem   **j. • Damascus**   **k. • Amman**
l. ⊕ **West Bank**   **m. Mediterranean Sea**   **n.** ⬭ **Dead Sea**

1. Locate Jordan, and color it brown.

2. Locate Israel, and color it blue.

3. Locate Egypt, and color it red.

4. Locate Lebanon, and color it orange.

Name: _____   Date: _____

Unit 10: Regions of Conflict

A. Conflict Between Countries—Israel and Palestine (cont.)

5. Locate Syria, and color it yellow.

6. Write Jerusalem by the dot and the letter "i."

7. Write Damascus by the dot and the letter "j."

8. Write Amman by the dot and the letter "k."

9. The Dead Sea is on the border between Israel and   a) Egypt   b) Lebanon
   c) Jordan   d) Saudi Arabia.

10. Located along the western border of Israel is the   a) Sea of Galilee
    b) Mediterranean Sea   c) Jordan River   d) Gulf of Aqaba.

MAP 22

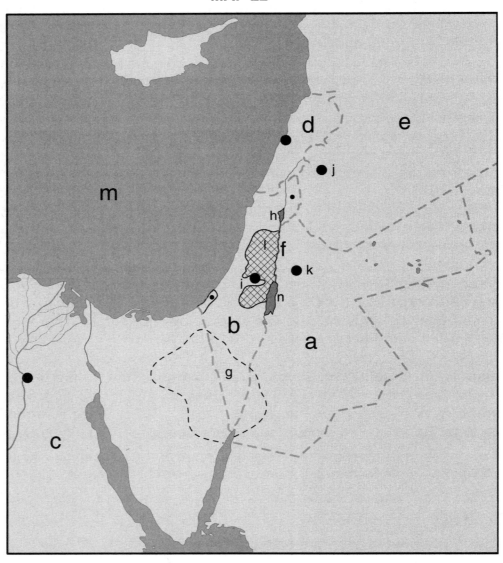

Name: _____   Date: _____

Unit 10: Regions of Conflict

B. Conflict Within Countries

1. The Balkan Peninsula

Read the following, and then complete the exercise that follows.

There has been a great deal of conflict among the countries located on the Balkan Peninsula. This area is located between the Adriatic and Ionian Seas on the west, and the Black and Aegean Seas on the east. Ethnic, religious, and boundary differences have fueled many of the conflicts. From Roman times, many different groups have entered the Balkan Peninsula. As the different groups came to the Balkans, they brought their own customs and culture. However, they also accepted customs from stronger rulers who controlled parts of the region. Religious differences resulted, as some groups came under the influence of the Catholic Church, while others followed the Islamic religion and some the Greek Orthodox Church.

A recent conflict resulted in the breakup of the country Yugoslavia, which had been a communist nation led by the dictator Marshal Josip Tito. The country under Tito was divided into republics. In these republics were many ethnic groups, such as Serbs, Croats, and Muslims. Under Tito's dictatorship, most of the ethnic groups lived peacefully, while maintaining their customs and religious differences.

When Tito died, civil war erupted, as many of the republics wanted to be independent from Yugoslavia. In the civil war that followed, many of the republics that had formed Yugoslavia had populations of both Croats and Serbs. The Croats wanted independence from Yugoslavia, while the Serbs wanted to remain part of Yugoslavia. As the political conflict between Croats and Serbs became greater, conflicts over ethnic differences resulted. One of the most brutal civil wars was fought in the Croatian province. The civil war in Croatia was repeated many times, as former republics fought for independence. Today, the former Yugoslavia has been divided into the countries of Slovenia, Croatia, Bosnia and Herzegovina, Montenegro, Serbia, Macedonia, and Kosovo.

Use **Map 23**, **Map 24**, and **an atlas** to complete the following. Each of the countries, cities, or physical features below is indicated on Map 23 by a lowercase letter.

**a. Hungary   b. Former Yugoslavia   c. Albania   d. Greece   e. Bulgaria
f. Romania   g. Adriatic Sea   h. Aegean Sea   i. Black Sea   j. Danube River**

1. Locate Hungary, and color it red.
2. Locate the former Yugoslavia, and color it brown.
3. Locate Albania, and color it green.
4. Locate Greece, and color it blue.
5. Locate Bulgaria, and color it orange.
6. Locate Romania, and color it yellow.

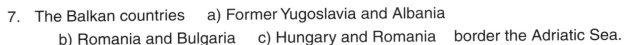

Unit 10: Regions of Conflict

B. Conflict Within Countries—The Balkan Peninsula (cont.)

7. The Balkan countries   a) Former Yugoslavia and Albania
   b) Romania and Bulgaria   c) Hungary and Romania   border the Adriatic Sea.

8. The Balkan countries   a) Romania and Albania   b) Hungary and Romania
   c) Romania and Bulgaria   border the Black Sea.

9. The Balkan country   a) Romania   b) Hungary   c) Albania   d) Greece
   borders the Aegean Sea.

10. Place a + on the blank if the Danube River flows through the country.
    ____ Hungary   ____ Macedonia   ____ Greece   ____ Romania

Map 24 shows the countries on the Balkan Peninsula **after** the civil war and breakup of Yugoslavia. Use **Map 24** and **an atlas** to complete the following. Each country, city, or physical feature is identified by a lowercase letter on the map.

**a. Slovenia   b. Croatia   c. Bosnia and Herzegovina   d. Serbia   e. Kosovo
f. Montenegro   g. Albania   h. Macedonia   i. Greece   j. Bulgaria   k. Romania
l. Hungary   m. Belgrade   n. Zagreb   o. Sofia   p. Bucharest   q. Adriatic Sea
r. Aegean Sea   s. Black Sea   t. Danube River**

1. Locate and color Slovenia brown.   2.   Locate and color Croatia light green.
3. Locate and color Bosnia and Herzegovina pink. 4. Locate and color Serbia gray.
5. Locate and color Kosovo light blue.   6.   Locate and color Albania dark green.
7. Locate and color Macedonia purple.   8.   Locate and color Montenegro peach.
9. Locate and color Greece dark blue.   10.   Locate and color Bulgaria orange.
11. Locate and color Romania yellow.   12.   Locate and color Hungary red.

13. Place a + on the blank if the country borders the Adriatic Sea.
    ____ Hungary   ____ Slovenia   ____ Albania ____ Bulgaria   ____ Croatia
    ____ Montenegro   ____ Bosnia and Herzegovina ____ Macedonia ____ Romania

14. Place a + on the blank if the country borders the Black Sea.
    ____ Hungary   ____ Slovenia   ____ Bulgaria   ____ Serbia   ____ Bosnia & Herz.
    ____ Macedonia ____ Romania   ____ Greece   ____ Croatia ____ Montenegro

15. Place a + on the blank if the country borders the Aegean Sea.
    ____ Bulgaria   ____ Croatia   ____ Macedonia   ____ Romania   ____ Greece

16. The letter "k" indicates the city   a) Zagreb   b) Sofia   c) Bucharest   d) Belgrade.
17. The letter "l" indicates the city   a) Zagreb   b) Sofia   c) Bucharest   d) Belgrade.
18. The letter "m" indicates the city   a) Zagreb   b) Sofia   c) Bucharest   d) Belgrade.
19. The letter "n" indicates the city   a) Zagreb   b) Sofia   c) Bucharest   d) Belgrade.

Name: _____ Date: _____

Unit 10: Regions of Conflict

B. Conflict Within Countries—The Balkan Peninsula (cont.)

MAP 23

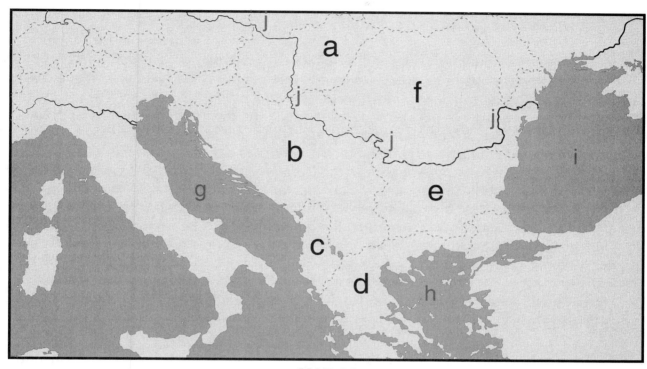

MAP 24

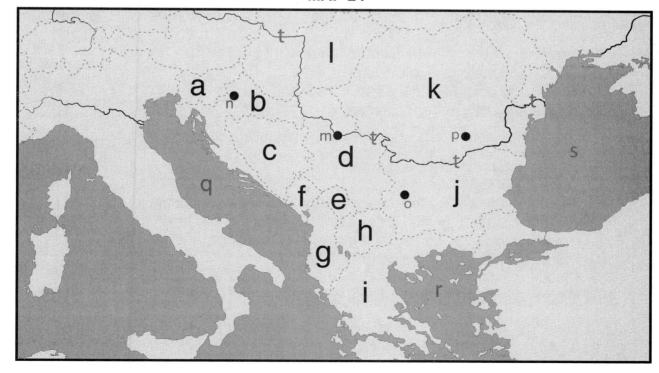

Unit 10: Regions of Conflict

B. Conflict Within Countries

2. Democratic Republic of the Congo

Read the following, and then complete the exercise that follows.

In many countries south of the Sahara Desert, civil war is waged between the government and various rebel groups trying to seize control of the country. In these civil wars, the average citizens have suffered the most, as their property has been taken by the rebels, their homes destroyed, their families separated, and their community services disrupted, leaving many without food and medicine. In many countries like the Democratic Republic of the Congo, the country has been under the control of a dictator who has done very little to improve life for the average person. In the Democratic Republic of the Congo, civil war has been waged as rebel groups struggle against the government and, in some cases, against each other. Some rebel groups have been supported by neighboring countries, such as Rwanda. The civil war has destroyed the economy of this large mineral-rich country. Life in the countryside and in the cities has been disrupted, and citizens find it very difficult to survive.

Use **Map 25** and **an atlas** to complete the following. Each of the countries, cities, or physical features below is indicated on Map 25 by a lowercase letter, a dot, or a symbol.

a. Democratic Republic of the Congo   b. Uganda   c. Rwanda   d. Burundi
e. Congo   f. Angola   i. Zambia   j. Tanzania   k. Kinshasa
l. Kampala   m. Kigali   n. Kisangani   o. Congo River   p. Equator

1.   Locate and color the Democratic Republic of the Congo red.
2.   Locate and color Uganda blue.
3.   Locate and color Rwanda green.
4.   Locate and color Burundi orange.
5.   Locate and color Congo brown.
6.   Locate and color Angola yellow.
7.   Locate and color Zambia purple.
8.   Locate and color Tanzania pink.
9.   Place the letter "k" by the dot that locates Kinshasa and label it.
10.   Place the letter "l" by the dot that locates Kampala and label it.
11.   Place the letter "m" by the dot that locates Kigali and label it.
12.   Place the letter "n" by the dot that locates Kisangani and label it.
13.   Place the letter "o" along the Congo River.
14.   Draw a line over the dashed line, and label it "equator 0°."

Name: _____   Date: _____

Unit 10: Regions of Conflict

B. Conflict Within Countries—Democratic Republic of the Congo (cont.)

MAP 25

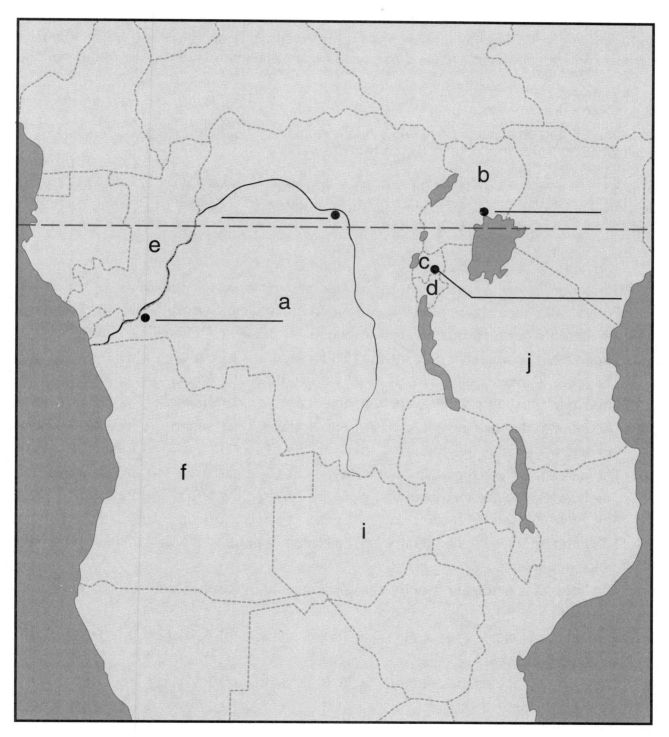

Unit 11: Strategically Important Countries in the Eastern Hemisphere

The countries of the Middle East, North Africa, Central Asia, and the Caucasus Mountains region must be considered strategically important countries. These countries are strategically important because many other countries of the world have a vital interest in each of these regions. The location, large oil reserves, the rapidly growing population with large numbers and a standard of living much below the more developed countries of the world, and factors such as climate and religion make these countries of vital interest to the rest of the world.

A. Location

Use **Map 26** and **an atlas** to complete the following. Each of the following countries has a strategic location. Circle the letter of the correct answer.

Algeria	Libya	Tunisia	Saudi Arabia	Yemen	Israel	Egypt
Jordan	Syria	Georgia	Turkmenistan	Turkey	Iran	Iraq
Tajikistan	Armenia	Uzbekistan	Kazakhstan	Azerbaijan	Kyrgyzstan	

1. The letter "a" locates the country   a) Algeria   b) Libya   c) Tunisia   d) Egypt.
2. The letter "b" locates the country   a) Algeria   b) Tunisia   c) Egypt   d) Libya.
3. The letter "c" locates the country   a) Algeria   b) Libya   c) Tunisia   d) Egypt.
4. The letter "d" locates the country   a) Algeria   b) Libya   c) Tunisia   d) Egypt.
5. The letter "e" locates the country   a) Saudi Arabia   b) Yemen   c) Israel   d) Jordan.
6. The letter "f" locates the country   a) Yemen   b) Saudi Arabia   c) Israel   d) Jordan.
7. The letter "g" locates the country   a) Saudi Arabia   b) Yemen   c) Israel   d) Jordan.
8. The letter "h" locates the country   a) Saudi Arabia   b) Yemen   c) Jordan   b) Israel.
9. The letter "i" locates the country   a) Syria   b) Iraq   c) Iran   d) Turkey.
10. The letter "j" locates the country   a) Syria   b) Iraq   c) Iran   d) Turkey.
11. The letter "k" locates the country   a) Syria   b) Iraq   c) Iran   d) Turkey.
12. The letter "l" locates the country   a) Syria   b) Iraq   c) Iran   d) Turkey.
13. The letter "m" locates the country   a) Tajikistan   b) Iran   c) Uzbekistan   d) Turkmenistan.
14. The letter "n" locates the country   a) Turkmenistan   b) Tajikistan   c) Uzbekistan   d) Iran.
15. The letter "o" locates the country   a) Turkmenistan   b) Tajikistan   c) Uzbekistan   d) Georgia.
16. The letter "p" locates the country   a) Turkmenistan   b) Tajikistan   c) Uzbekistan   d) Kyrgyzstan.

Unit 11: Strategically Important Countries in the Eastern Hemisphere

A. Location (cont.)

17. The letter "q" locates the country   a) Kazakhstan   b) Georgia   c) Armenia
    d) Azerbaijan.

18. The letter "r" locates the country   a) Kazakhstan   b) Georgia   c) Armenia
    d) Azerbaijan.

19. The letter "s" locates the country   a) Kazakhstan   b) Georgia   c) Armenia
    d) Azerbaijan.

20. The letter "t" locates the country   a) Kazakhstan   b) Georgia   c) Armenia
    d) Azerbaijan.

21. Complete the chart below. Write the name of the continent where the country is located
    on the blank by each country. Place a plus (+) on the blank to show the region where the
    country is located.

Country	Continent	Middle East	North Africa	Central Asia	Caucasus Region
a. Algeria	_____	_____	_____	_____	_____
b. Libya	_____	_____	_____	_____	_____
c. Tunisia	_____	_____	_____	_____	_____
d. Egypt	_____	_____	_____	_____	_____
e. Saudi Arabia	_____	_____	_____	_____	_____
f. Yemen	_____	_____	_____	_____	_____
g. Israel	_____	_____	_____	_____	_____
h. Jordan	_____	_____	_____	_____	_____
i. Syria	_____	_____	_____	_____	_____
j. Iraq	_____	_____	_____	_____	_____
k. Iran	_____	_____	_____	_____	_____
l. Turkey	_____	_____	_____	_____	_____
m. Turkmenistan	_____	_____	_____	_____	_____
n. Tajikistan	_____	_____	_____	_____	_____
o. Uzbekistan	_____	_____	_____	_____	_____
p. Kyrgyzstan	_____	_____	_____	_____	_____
q. Kazakhstan	_____	_____	_____	_____	_____
r. Georgia	_____	_____	_____	_____	_____
s. Armenia	_____	_____	_____	_____	_____
t. Azerbaijan	_____	_____	_____	_____	_____

Name: _____   Date: _____

Unit 11: Strategically Important Countries in the Eastern Hemisphere

A. Location (cont.)

MAP 26

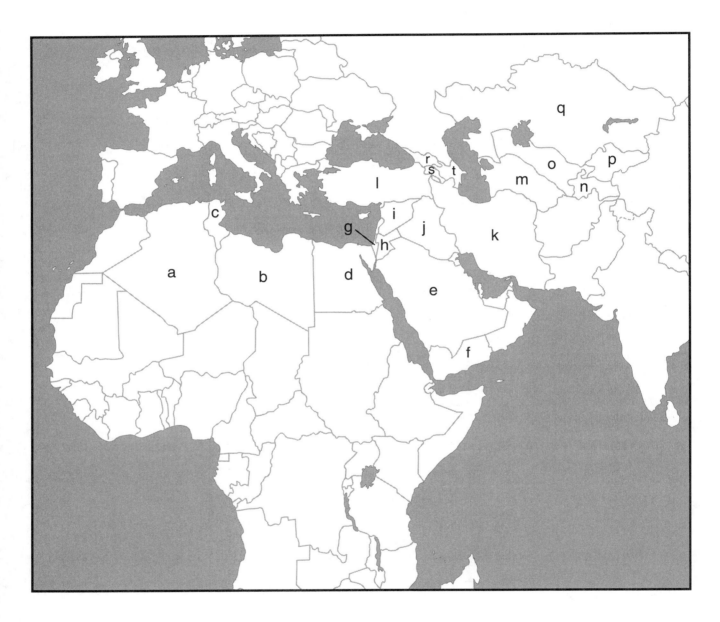

Name: _____ Date: _____

Unit 11: Strategically Important Countries in the Eastern Hemisphere

B. Oil Reserves

1. Use **Map 27** and **an atlas** to complete the following. The symbol ![symbol] indicates the location of countries with large reserves of oil in North Africa, the Middle East, Central Asia, and the Caucasus Region. Place a plus (+) on the blank if the country has large oil reserves.

_____ a. Algeria   _____ b. Libya   _____ c. Tunisia   _____ d. Egypt

_____ e. Saudi Arabia   _____ f. Yemen   _____ g. Israel   _____ h. Jordan

_____ i. Syria   _____ j. Iraq   _____ k. Iran   _____ l. Turkey

_____ m. Turkmenistan   _____ n. Tajikistan   _____ o. Uzbekistan

_____ p. Kazakhstan   _____ q. Georgia   _____ r. Armenia

_____ s. Azerbaijan

MAP 27

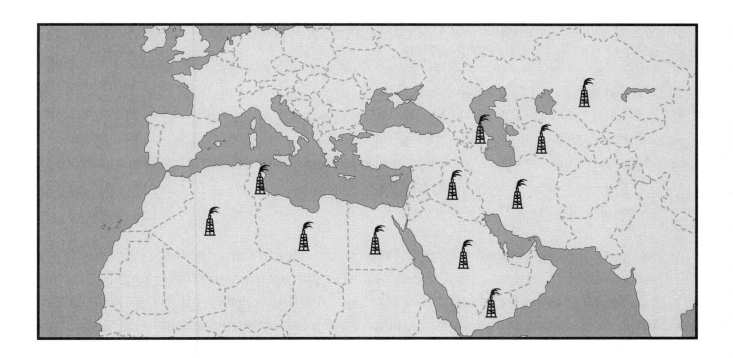

Unit 11: Strategically Important Countries in the Eastern Hemisphere

B. Oil Reserves (cont.)

Read the following, and then complete the exercise that follows.

The United States, Western Europe, and Japan use enormous quantities of oil. All of these countries must import a large part of their oil needs from North Africa and the Middle East. Recently, the reserves of oil in the Caucasus Region and Central Asia are becoming more important as a source of oil for the United States, Western Europe, and Japan. Ocean tankers carrying shipments of oil to the United States, Western Europe, and Japan must travel the Mediterranean Sea, Indian Ocean, Persian Gulf, and Black Sea to deliver the oil to the importing countries.

Use **Map 28** and **an atlas** to complete the following.

1. The letter "a" locates the   a) Mediterranean Sea   b) Black Sea   c) Caspian Sea
    d) Persian Gulf   e) Indian Ocean.

2. The letter "b" locates the   a) Mediterranean Sea   b) Black Sea   c) Caspian Sea
    d) Persian Gulf   e) Indian Ocean.

3. The letter "c" locates the   a) Mediterranean Sea   b) Black Sea   c) Caspian Sea
    d) Persian Gulf   e) Indian Ocean.

4. The letter "d" locates the   a) Mediterranean Sea   b) Black Sea   c) Caspian Sea
    d) Persian Gulf   e) Indian Ocean.

5. The letter "f" locates the   a) Mediterranean Sea   b) Black Sea   c) Caspian Sea
    d) Persian Gulf   e) Indian Ocean.

6. Ocean tankers enter the Persian Gulf from the   a) Indian Ocean   b) Black Sea
    c) Mediterranean Sea   d) Caspian Sea.

7. As ocean tankers steam into or out of the Persian Gulf, nearby countries include
    a) Israel and Turkey   b) Saudi Arabia and Egypt   c) Iran and Saudi Arabia
    d) Tajikistan and Kazakhstan.

8. Connect the dotted line to show the route of a pipeline that is being built to deliver oil from Central Asia and the Caucasus Region.

9. The dashed line shows the route that oil tankers must take to transport the oil from the Caucasus Region and Central Asia. Place a plus (+) on the blank if the oil tanker must pass through the location to transport the oil. Begin at "A" on the dashed line.

____ Strait of Gibraltar   ____ Caspian Sea   ____ Mediterranean Sea   ____ Aegean Sea

____ North Sea   ____ Dardanelles   ____ Sea of Marmara   ____ Red Sea

____ Bosporus   ____ Black Sea

Unit 11: Strategically Important Countries in the Eastern Hemisphere

B. Oil Reserves (cont.)

MAP 28

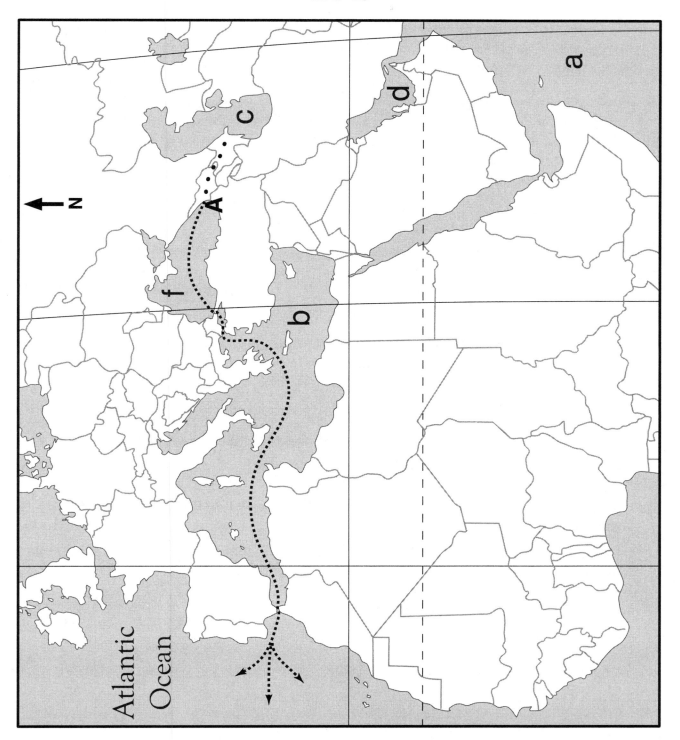

Name: _____   Date: _____

Unit 11: Strategically Important Countries in the Eastern Hemisphere

C. Religion

Read the following, and then complete the exercise that follows.

In North African and Middle Eastern countries, most people belong to the Islamic religion. Those who belong to the Islamic religion are referred to as Muslims. Most who belong to the Islamic religion are members of either the Sunni or Shi'ite sects. Israel and Lebanon are countries in the Middle East that do not have a majority of people who are Islamic. In Israel the majority of people practice Judaism (Jewish), and in Lebanon, the majority are Christian.

In Central Asia, all countries except Kazakhstan have a clear majority of people who are Islamic. In Kazakhstan, the majority is Islamic, but a large number of people belong to the Russian Orthodox Christian Church.

Armenia, Azerbaijan, and Georgia are in the Caucasus region. A majority of the people of Azerbaijan are Islamic. In Armenia and Georgia, the majority are either Armenian Orthodox or Georgian Orthodox Christian.

Use **Map 29a**, **Map 29b**, and **an atlas** to complete the following. Each of the religions listed below is shown on the maps with a lowercase letter inside the boundary of the country. If the letter is inside a country boundary, it means a majority of the population are members of that religious group.

a. Islam   **b. Judaism**   **c. Russian Orthodox Christian,**
                                              Armenian Orthodox Christian,
d. Christian   **Georgian Orthodox Christian**

1. Place a plus (+) on the blank if the majority of the population are members of Islam.
    ____ Algeria   ____ Georgia   ____ Egypt   ____ Iran   ____ Iraq   ____ Israel
    ____ Armenia   ____ Saudi Arabia   ____ Jordan   ____ Syria   ____ Libya
    ____ Tunisia   ____ Azerbaijan   ____ Kazakhstan   ____ Tajikistan
    ____ Turkmenistan   ____ Uzbekistan

2. Place a plus (+) on the blank if the majority of the population are members of Judaism.
    ____ Algeria   ____ Georgia   ____ Egypt   ____ Iran   ____ Iraq   ____ Israel
    ____ Armenia   ____ Jordan   ____ Syria   ____ Kazakhstan   ____ Lebanon

3. Place a plus (+) on the blank if the majority of the population are members of an Orthodox religious group.
    ____ Algeria   ____ Georgia   ____ Egypt   ____ Israel   ____ Armenia   ____ Jordan
    ____ Syria   ____ Libya   ____ Tunisia   ____ Azerbaijan   ____ Kazakhstan
    ____ Tajikistan   ____ Turkmenistan   ____ Uzbekistan   ____ Lebanon

Name: _____ Date: _____

Unit 11: Strategically Important Countries in the Eastern Hemisphere

C. Religion (cont.)

4. Place a plus (+) on the blank if the majority of the population are Christians.

_____ Algeria _____ Armenia _____ Georgia _____ Egypt _____ Iran _____ Iraq
_____ Israel _____ Saudi Arabia _____ Jordan _____ Syria _____ Azerbaijan
_____ Kazakhstan _____ Tajikistan _____ Turkmenistan _____ Lebanon

MAP 29

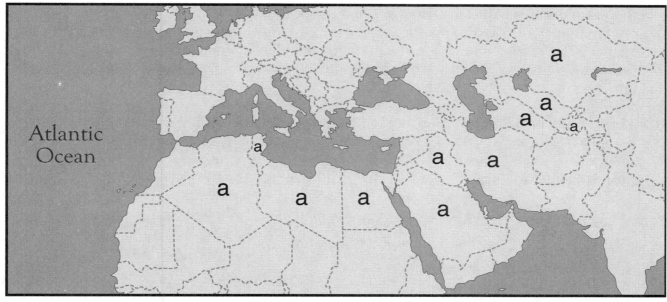

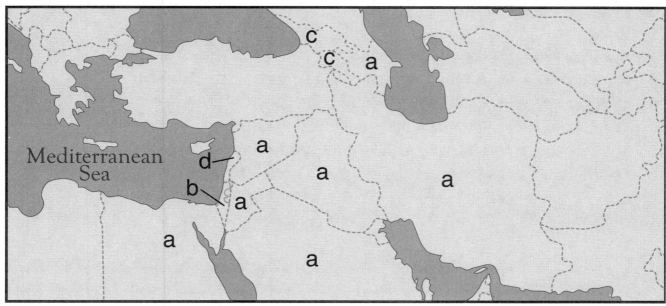

Unit 11: Strategically Important Countries in the Eastern Hemisphere

C. Religion (cont.)

Read the following, and then complete the exercise that follows.

Jerusalem is a city with religious importance to Christians, Jews, and Muslims (Islam). For Christians and Jews, Jerusalem is a holy city associated with the original temple and the crucifixion of Jesus. It is from the teachings of the Bible that Christians and Jews derive their religious practices. To the Islamic people, Jerusalem is of religious significance because they believe that it was from Jerusalem that Mohammed, the founder of the Islamic religion, went to heaven. Mecca in Saudi Arabia is the holiest city for the Islamic people. It is in Mecca that the shrine toward which all Muslims kneel and pray is located.

Mohammed, the founder of the Islamic religion, grew up in the city of Medina where he was raised by a prosperous uncle. Later in life, the teachings found in the Koran, the holy book for Muslims, were revealed to him. To escape persecution, he fled from Medina to Mecca, which became the holy city for Islam.

Use **Map 30** and **an atlas** to complete the following.

a. Mecca	**b. Jerusalem**	**c. Medina**	**d. Red Sea**	**e. Sea of Galilee**
f. Jordan River	**g. Israel**	**h. Saudi Arabia**		

1. Place the letter "a" by the dot that locates Mecca.
2. Place the letter "b" by the dot that locates Jerusalem.
3. Place the letter "c" by the dot that locates Medina.
4. Place the letter "d" on the Red Sea.
5. Place the letter "e" on the Sea of Galilee.
6. Place the letter "f" along the Jordan River.
7. Place the letter "g" on the country Israel.
8. Place the letter "h" on the country Saudi Arabia.
9. Mecca and Medina are holy cities for the   a) Jews   b) Christians   c) Muslims.
10. The holy book for Christians is the   a) Bible   b) Koran.
11. The holy book for the Muslims is the   a) Bible   b) Koran.
12. The holy city for Christians and Jews is   a) Mecca   b) Medina   c) Jerusalem.

Unit 11: Strategically Important Countries in the Eastern Hemisphere

C. Religion (cont.)

MAP 30

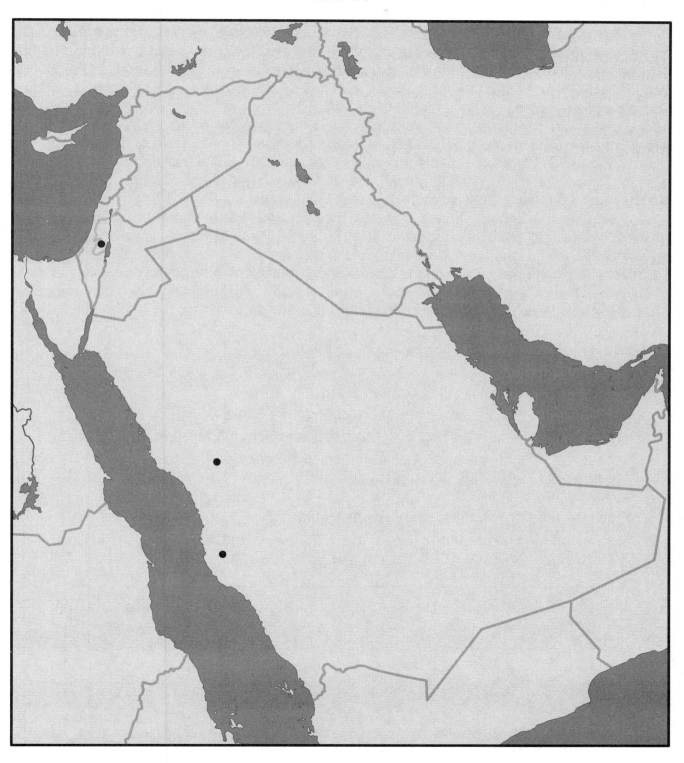

Name: _____   Date: _____

Unit 12: Man and the Environment

A. Desertification

Read the following, and then complete the exercise that follows.

     The environment in many parts of the world is very fragile. It is in the dry regions of the Eastern Hemisphere that the activities of man have been the most destructive to the natural environment. In many areas, man's efforts to irrigate the desert land have resulted in "desertification." This term is used to refer to those dry lands where the environment has been altered, with a resulting increase in the amount of desert.

     In some dry regions, desertification occurs when man, wind, and deficient rainfall have caused the destruction of the natural environment. This has been the case where animals have overgrazed the short-grass region surrounding the desert. The overgrazing removed the short grasses, and in years of deficient rainfall, the winds blow away large amounts of topsoil. This results in an increase in the size of the desert.

     South of the Sahara Desert, a region known as the **Sahel** was a broad band of short grasses where nomadic people grazed their animals. Although the region was dry and the grasses were sparse, it did provide grazing for the animals. Overgrazing during exceptionally dry years resulted in the destruction of the sparse short grasses and the Sahel becoming a part of the Sahara Desert. The size of the Sahara Desert has actually been increased by overgrazing the Sahel during years that were drier than normal.

Use **Map 31** to complete the following.

1. When desertification occurs, the area of the desert   a) becomes smaller
   b) remains the same   c) becomes larger.

2. Desertification is a problem in areas bordering the Sahara Desert because of
   a) too many animals grazing the short grassland bordering the desert in dry years
   b) too few animals grazing the short grassland in dry years
   c) development of cities in the region.

3. The region of short grasses bordering the Sahara where desertification is a problem is
   called   a) the Swahili   b) the savanna   c) the Sahel.

MAP 31

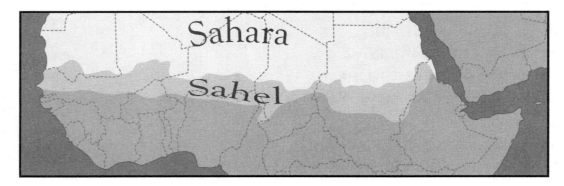

Name: _____   Date: _____

Unit 12: Man and the Environment

B. Salinization

Read the following, and then complete the exercise that follows.

The Amu Darya River and Syr Darya River had flowed for centuries from the mountains into the landlocked Aral Sea. The water level of this landlocked sea has been dependent on the yearly flow of water from the rivers.

Today, water from the Amu Darya River and Syr Darya River has been diverted to irrigate the Kyzylkum and Karakum Deserts to grow crops like cotton and vegetables. The water used for irrigating the desert is no longer available to maintain the level of the Aral Sea. As a result, the Aral Sea is shrinking in size and becoming much saltier. The fishing industry that once flourished has been jeopardized. As water continues to be diverted from the Amu Darya and Syr Darya Rivers, the Aral Sea will continue to shrink in size. As the Aral Sea shrinks, the exposed shoreline of salt-laden soil increases the area of the desert.

A particular problem in the irrigated lands of the Kyzylkum and Karakum Deserts is salinization. In these dry, hot deserts, the humidity level is low, so evaporation of water occurs rapidly. When the water used for irrigation evaporates, it leaves behind the salts that are contained in the water. The salts accumulate over time and make it impossible to grow crops in the desert soil, which has become crusted with a layer of salt. This is a problem faced in all parts of the world where dry lands have been irrigated.

Use **Map 32** and **an atlas** to complete the following.

Amu Darya   Syr Darya   Aral Sea   Kyzylkum   Karakum   Uzbekistan
Turkmenistan   Kazakhstan

1. The letter "a" locates the   a) Amu Darya River   b) Syr Darya River   c) Kyzylkum Desert
    d) Karakum Desert.
2. The letter "b" locates the   a) Amu Darya River   b) Syr Darya River   c) Kyzylkum Desert
    d) Karakum Desert.
3. The letter "c" locates the   a) Amu Darya River   b) Syr Darya River   c) Kyzylkum Desert
    d) Karakum Desert.
4. The letter "d" locates the   a) Amu Darya River   b) Syr Darya River   c) Kyzylkum Desert
    d) Karakum Desert.
5. The letter "e" locates the country   a) Uzbekistan   b) Turkmenistan   c) Kazakhstan.
6. The letter "f" locates the country   a) Uzbekistan   b) Turkmenistan   c) Kazakhstan.
7. The letter "g" locates the country   a) Uzbekistan   b) Turkmenistan   c) Kazakhstan.
8. The Kyzlkum Desert is located in   a) Uzbekistan   b) Turkmenistan   c) Kazakhstan.
9. The Karakum Desert is located in   a) Uzbekistan   b) Turkmenistan   c) Kazakhstan.

Name: _____   Date: _____

Unit 12: Man and the Environment

B. Salinization (cont.)

10. The Syr Darya River flows across   a) Uzbekistan   b) Turkmenistan   c) Kazakhstan.

11. The Amu Darya River flows across   a) Uzbekistan and Turkmenistan
    b) Turkmenistan and Kazakhstan   c) Uzbekistan and Kazakhstan   and into the Aral Sea.

12. Uzbekistan, Turkmenistan, and Kazakhstan are countries in   a) the Middle East
    b) Africa   c) Central Asia.

MAP 32

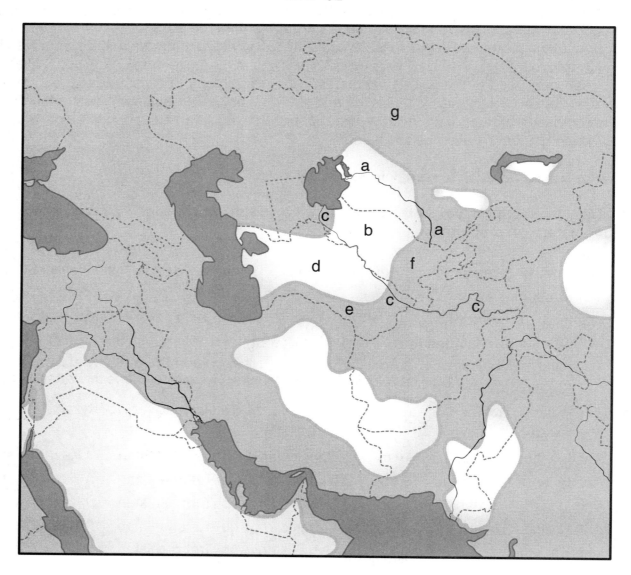

Name: _____ Date: _____

Unit 12: Man and the Environment

C. Flooding

Read the following, and then complete the exercise that follows.

    In the Eastern Hemisphere, the Nile River in Egypt and the Huang Ho (Yellow) River in China are two major rivers where floods were common in years past. When in flood stage, the large fertile floodplains, on which lived large numbers of people, were underwater. To protect the floodplains from flooding, levees have been built. The levees have prevented the loss of crops that grow on the floodplain. However, the fertile soil carried by the river is no longer deposited on the floodplain to enrich the soil. Farmers must now add fertilizer to grow the abundant crops. The fertilizer increases the cost to produce crops. The runoff of the fertilizer also contaminates waterways, where many people fish and obtain their drinking water.

    Now, the rivers are confined between the levees, and the soil carried by the river is deposited in the river, rather than on the floodplain. This results in the bed of the river gradually rising above the surrounding floodplain. Like other large rivers around the world where levees have been constructed, it has been necessary to build ever-higher levees along the Nile and Huang Ho Rivers.

MAP 33a

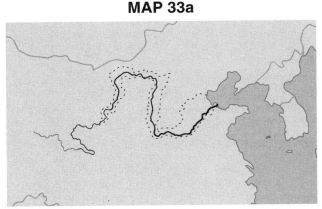

Use **Map 33a** and **an atlas** to complete the following.

1. The Huang Ho River is shown with a wavy line. Place the letter "a" along the river.
2. Connect the dashes to indicate the floodplain region near the Huang Ho River.
3. Color the region inside the dashes green.

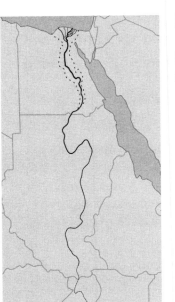

MAP 33b

Use **Map 33b** and **an atlas** to complete the following.

1. The Nile River is shown with a wavy line. Place the letter "b" along the river.
2. Connect the dashes to indicate the floodplain region near the river.
3. Color the region inside the dashes green.

Name: _____ Date: _____

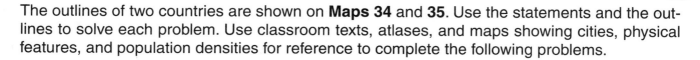

Unit 13: Solve These Problems

PROBLEM 1

The outlines of two countries are shown on **Maps 34** and **35**. Use the statements and the outlines to solve each problem. Use classroom texts, atlases, and maps showing cities, physical features, and population densities for reference to complete the following problems.

    The countries outlined below are located on the same continent. The countries are identified as Country A and Country B. One is a developed country, the other is underdeveloped.

    When analyzing the difference between developed and underdeveloped countries, it is important to compare such factors as the percent of population engaged in subsistence agriculture, the education level of the population, the per capita GNP, the percent of the economy that is devoted to manufacturing and industry, life span, and inflation.

Map 34: Country A (Developed Country)

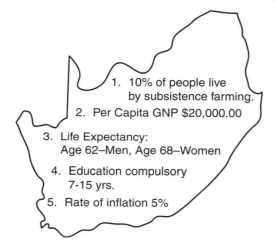

1. 10% of people live by subsistence farming.
2. Per Capita GNP $20,000.00
3. Life Expectancy: Age 62–Men, Age 68–Women
4. Education compulsory 7-15 yrs.
5. Rate of inflation 5%

Map 35: Country B (Underdeveloped Country)

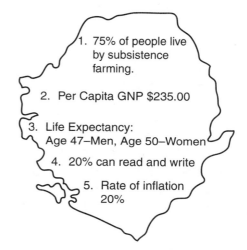

1. 75% of people live by subsistence farming.
2. Per Capita GNP $235.00
3. Life Expectancy: Age 47–Men, Age 50–Women
4. 20% can read and write
5. Rate of inflation 20%

1. The name of Country A is a) Kenya b) South Africa c) Mozambique d) Sierra Leone.
2. The name of Country B is a) Kenya b) South Africa c) Mozambique d) Sierra Leone.

Label each statement with the country name, South Africa or Sierra Leone.

3. _____ Most of the population's livelihood depends on subsistence agriculture.

4. _____ Most of the population works in industry and manufacturing.

5. _____ Life expectancy is 65 years or more.

6. _____ Life expectancy is 50 years or less.

7. _____ Few people can read and write.

8. _____ Most people can read and write.

9. _____ Standard of living is very low.

10. _____ Standard of living is high.

Name: _____   Date: _____

Unit 13: Solve These Problems

PROBLEM 1 (cont.)

Read the following, and then complete the exercise that follows.

  Almost all countries experience some inflation. **Inflation** occurs when the prices charged for goods and services increase. In developed countries, the rate of income increase for most of the population is equal to or greater than the rate of inflation. This means that the standard of living for people in the developed countries is increasing or holding steady. However, in underdeveloped countries, most people do not have jobs that produce income. Most of the people depend on subsistence agriculture to live. They have very little to sell for cash. Yet, it is in the underdeveloped countries that some of the highest rates of inflation are found.

  Example: The price for a pound of meat is $1.00, and the inflation rate is 20% yearly. A pound of meat that is $1.00 today will be $1.20 next year. In underdeveloped countries, the rate of inflation often changes daily or weekly. If the inflation rate is 20% and it changes daily, then a pound of meat that costs $1.00 today will cost $1.20 tomorrow.

  Person A is living in an underdeveloped country, and the inflation rate is 20% monthly. To buy food supplies for the family requires $20.00 per month. Living in an underdeveloped country, Person A's total income is $500 per year. This $500 is the amount of money that is available for all family expenses.

1. Complete the following chart for the seventh and eighth month.

Month	Cost	*	$ Inflation Rate	=	Increase per Month	Cost	Total Spent
1.	$20.00	*	0.20		$ 4.00	$24.00	$24.00
2.	$24.00	*	0.20		$ 4.80	$28.80	$52.80
3.	$28.80	*	0.20		$ 5.76	$34.56	$87.36
4.	$34.56	*	0.20		$ 6.91	$41.47	$128.83
5.	$41.47	*	0.20		$ 8.29	$49.76	$178.59
6.	$49.76	*	0.20		$ 9.95	$59.71	$238.30
7.	$59.71	*	0.20		$11.94	_____	_____
8.	$_____	*	_____		_____	_____	_____

Use the above chart to answer the following questions.

2. During the eight-month period, the amount of money needed to buy the family food supply has a) not changed b) become less c) more than doubled.

3. During the eight-month period, the amount of money spent on food is approximately
  a) one-half b) one-fourth c) three-fourths of the total yearly income.

4. At the end of the eighth month, the amount of money the family will have available will be approximately a) $200 b) $300 c) $100.

5. At the rate of inflation and with the total yearly income, this family a) will b) will not have enough money to buy food for the year.

Name: _____   Date: _____

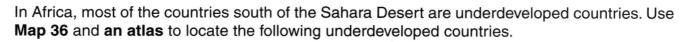

Unit 13: Solve These Problems

PROBLEM 2

In Africa, most of the countries south of the Sahara Desert are underdeveloped countries. Use **Map 36** and **an atlas** to locate the following underdeveloped countries.

Chad	Niger	Western Sahara	Mali	Burkina Faso	Benin
Guinea-Bissau		Senegal	Angola	Mozambique	Tanzania
Zambia					

1. The letter "a" locates the country a) Chad   b) Mozambique   c) Mali   d) Senegal.
2. The letter "b" locates the country a) Chad   b) Mozambique   c) Malawi   d) Senegal.
3. The letter "c" locates the country a) Western Sahara   b) Burkina Faso   c) Benin
    d) Niger.
4. The letter "d" locates the country a) Western Sahara   b) Burkina Faso   c) Benin
    d) Angola.
5. The letter "e" locates the country a) Tanzania   b) Burkina Faso c) Benin   d) Angola.
6. The letter "f" locates the country a) Tanzania   b) Burkina Faso c) Benin   d) Angola.
7. The letter "g" locates the country a) Western Sahara   b) Burkina Faso   c) Benin
    d) Niger.
8. The letter "h" locates the country a) Tanzania   b) Burkina Faso c) Benin   d) Angola.
9. The letter "i" locates the country a) Zambia b) Mozambique   c) Guinea-Bissau
    d) Senegal.
10. The letter "j" locates the country a) Zambia b) Mozambique   c) Guinea-Bissau
    d) Senegal.
11. The letter "k" locates the country a) Niger   b) Chad   c) Zambia   d) Tanzania.
12. The letter "l" locates the country a) Chad   b) Senegal   c) Niger   d) Malawi.

Use the data in Problem 1 to complete the following.

13. Place a plus (+) on the blank by the statement that describes these underdeveloped countries.

_____ a. The per capita GNP is more than $1,000 per year.

_____ b. Fifty percent or more of the population depends on subsistence agriculture to live.

_____ c. The life span would be 68 years or older.

_____ d. The level of literacy would be very high when compared to developed countries.

_____ e. The inflation rate would often be greater than 20%.

Name: _____ Date: _____

Unit 13: Solve These Problems

PROBLEM 2 (cont.)

_____ f.   Unrest and civil wars are common.

_____ g.   Manufacturing is well-developed and employs many people.

_____ h.   The life span age would be less than 50 years.

_____ i.   The per capita GNP is less than $500.

_____ j.   Most people would have adequate health services available.

_____ k.   The literacy level would be very low when compared to developed countries.

14.   On your own paper, summarize how underdeveloped countries are unlike developed countries.

MAP 36

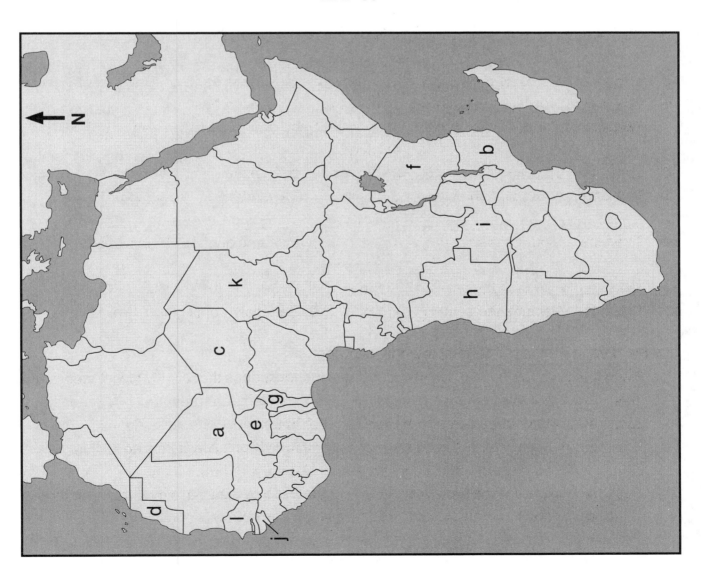

Name: _____   Date: _____

Unit 13: Solve These Problems

PROBLEM 3

On **Table I** and **Table II** below, the data is listed for two locations in the Eastern Hemisphere with the same climate type. The data in Table I and Table II shows the average monthly temperatures and rainfall for the climate. In answering the questions, it is important to remember that Table I and Table II represent the same climate type. The data in one table is for a Southern Hemisphere location, and the data in the other table is for a Northern Hemisphere location.

Table I

	J	F	M	A	M	J	J	A	S	O	N	D	Year
Temp. (°F)	49	51	53	54	56	57	57	58	60	59	56	51	55 ave.
Rainfall (in.)	4.8	3.6	3.1	1.0	0.7	0.1	0.0	0.0	0.3	1.0	2.4	4.6	22.2 T

Use **Table I** to answer the following questions.

1. The three months with the warmest average monthly temperatures are   a) January, February, March   b) November, December, January   c) August, September, October.
2. The three months with the lowest average monthly rainfall are   a) June, July, August   b) January, February, March   c) November, December, January.
3. The three months with the coolest average temperatures are   a) November, December, January   b) December, January, February   c) May, June, July.
4. The three months with the highest average monthly rainfall are   a) November, December, January   b) October, November, December   c) December, January, February.

Table II

	J	F	M	A	M	J	J	A	S	O	N	D	Year
Temp. (°F)	68	68	66	64	60	57	53	56	58	60	63	67	62 ave.
Rainfall (in.)	0.5	0.5	1.0	1.7	3.0	4.0	3.4	3.5	2.1	1.4	0.9	0.5	22.5 T

Use **Table II** to answer the following questions.

1. The three months with the warmest average monthly temperatures are   a) January, February, March   b) December, January, February   c) June, July, August.
2. The three months with the lowest average monthly rainfall are   a) June, July, August   b) January, February, March   c) December, January, February.
3. The three months with the coolest average temperatures are   a) November, December, January   b) December, January, February   c) June, July, August.
4. The three months with the highest average monthly rainfall are   a) November, December, January   b) June, July, August   c) December, January, February.

Name: _____ Date: _____

Unit 13: Solve These Problems

PROBLEM 3 (cont.)

Use both **Table I** and **Table II** to complete the following questions. Before continuing, review the characteristics of the following climates found in Chapter 7: semiarid, west coast marine, and Mediterranean.

The data for Table I and Table II is for the same climate type. One is for a Southern Hemisphere location, and the other table is for a Northern Hemisphere location.

Table I

1. The data for Table I is for the climate   a) semiarid   b) west coast marine
   c) Mediterranean.
2. The data for Table I is for a location in the   a) Northern Hemisphere
   b) Southern Hemisphere.
3. The summer months are   a) December, January, February
   b) November, December, January   c) June, July, August.
4. The winter months are   a) December, January, February
   b) November, December, January   c) June, July, August.
5. The summers in this climate are   a) warm and dry   b) warm and wet   c) cool and wet
   d) cool and dry.
6. The winters in this climate are   a) warm and dry   b) warm and wet   c) cool and wet
   d) cool and dry.

Table II

1. The data for Table II is for the climate   a) semiarid   b) west coast marine
   c) Mediterranean.
2. The data for Table II is for a location in the   a) Northern Hemisphere
   b) Southern Hemisphere.
3. The summer months are   a) December, January, February
   b) November, December, January   c) June, July, August.
4. The winter months are   a) December, January, February
   b) November, December, January   c) June, July, August.
5. The summers in this climate are   a) warm and dry   b) warm and wet   c) cool and wet
   d) cool and dry.
6. The winters in this climate are   a) warm and dry   b) warm and wet   c) cool and wet
   d) cool and dry.

Name: _____   Date: _____

Unit 13: Solve These Problems

PROBLEM 4

Before continuing, review the Chapter 12 material relating to irrigation of the Karakum and Kyzylkum Deserts in Central Asia.

Read the following, and then complete the exercise that follows.

In many regions of the Eastern Hemisphere, the climate is semiarid or desert. Because there is a need to produce food for the population, many countries have irrigated the semiarid and desert lands to produce food. When man changes the natural environment to irrigate semiarid or desert lands, there are often unforeseen problems.

In many of these semiarid and desert regions, man has used water from rivers to irrigate the land. In other regions, the irrigation has been accomplished by using water from aquifers. An **aquifer** is an underground rock structure where water has collected for thousands of years. The water enters the underground rock at a place "a," where the rock structure is close to the surface. There is a yearly supply of water that enters the aquifer. In the diagram to the right, the source of water is the rain and melted snow that flow down from the mountain and sink into the aquifer. Once in the aquifer, the water may travel hundreds of miles as it slowly seeps along. The water that is being taken from the well at "b" to irrigate the desert could be water that hundreds of years ago was rain and snow melt from the mountains.

50 million gallons of rain and snow melt enter the aquifer each year.

a

Each well uses 5 million gallons of water each year.

b

The desert land at "b" will be irrigated, using the water from the aquifer. The desert land at "b" is very dry. Crops can be grown on the desert with the irrigation. However, salinization does become a problem, as salt from the water builds up on the land.

Men realize that with more water, crops could be grown on the desert land and exported to other countries. However, to increase the amount of irrigated land, it is necessary to have more wells drilled into the aquifer and additional water pulled to the surface for irrigation. Each new well takes five million gallons of water from the aquifer each year.

1. When the number of wells is   a) 20   b) 40   c) 10   d) 50,   the amount of water taken from the aquifer will equal the amount coming into the aquifer at "a" each year.

2. If the number of wells is greater than   a) 20   b) 40   c) 10   d) 50, the amount of water in the aquifer will decrease.

Answer Keys

Unit 1: Political Geography of Eastern Hemisphere
A. Continents (p. 3)
Teacher check Map 1.

B. Countries
Teacher check Maps 2 and 3.
Map 2 Activity (p. 3–4)

a. AS/E	b. AF	c. E	d. AS
e. E	f. E	g. AF	h. AS
i. AS	j. AF	k. AS	l. AS
m. AS	n. AF	o. AF	p. AF
q. AF	r. AF	s. AF	t. AF
u. AF	v. AS	w. AS	x. AS
y. AS	z. AS/E	aa. AF	bb. AF

Map 3 Activity (p. 5)

a. Asia	b. Asia	c. Europe	d. Europe
e. Africa	f. Africa	g. Asia	h. Asia
i. Asia	j. Europe	k. Europe	l. Europe
m. Asia	n. Africa	o. Africa	p. Africa
q. Africa			

1. Map 3 countries are landlocked; or Map 2 countries have access to the seas.
2. The countries on Map 2 have access to seas without crossing a neighboring country.

C. Pretest (p. 7)

1. Asia	2. Africa	3. Africa
4. Europe	5. Africa	6. Asia
7. Asia	8. Europe	9. Asia
10. Asia	11. Asia, Europe	12. Asia
13. Asia	14. Asia	15. Africa
16. Asia	17. Asia	18. Europe
19. Europe	20. Asia	21. Asia
22. Europe	23. Africa	24. Australia
25. Asia	26. Europe, Asia	27. Africa
28. Africa	29. Europe	30. Europe

C. Test (p. 8)

1. Africa	2. Europe	3. Africa
4. Africa	5. Europe	6. Asia
7. Europe	8. Australia	9. Asia
10. Asia	11. Europe	12. Africa
13. Europe, Asia	14. Asia	15. Europe
16. Asia	17. Asia	18. Africa
19. Asia	20. Asia	21. Asia
22. Europe	23. Africa	24. Asia
25. Europe		

Unit 2: Population and Area
A. Population (p. 9–11)
Teacher check Map 4.

1. b	2. a	3. a
4a. Asia	b. Asia	c. Asia
d. Europe	e. Asia	f. Asia
g. Asia	h. Africa	i. Europe
j. Asia	k. Asia	l. Africa
m. Asia	n. Asia	o. Africa
p. Asia	q. Europe	r. Africa
s. Asia	t. Africa	

5. All should have plus signs.
Teacher check graph.

C. Population Density (p. 12–13)

1.	a. 1, 2, 139	b.	2, 3, 360
	c. 3, 5, 122	d.	7, 1, 8
	e. 4, 11, 211	f.	5; 20; 1,139
	g. 8, 15, 336	h.	6, 10, 171
	i. 11, 16, 238	j.	9, 19, 313
	k. 10, 17, 261	l.	13, 9, 79
	m. 15, 12, 93	n.	14, 6, 46
	o. 17, 14, 125	p.	12, 8, 70
	q. 18, 18, 199	r.	19, 13, 74
	s. 16, 4, 429	t.	20, 7, 41
2.	c		

Unit 3: More About Cities
A. The Function of Cities (p.14–17)
1. Teacher check Map 4.

1a. England	b. Norway	c. Italy
d. Russia	e. Russia	f. Germany
g. Turkey	h. Greece	i. Netherlands
j. Denmark	k. Japan	l. India
m. Egypt	n. China	o. Philippines
p. Singapore	q. Indonesia	r. Australia
s. China	t. Australia	

2. Teacher check Map 5.

2a. Hungary	b. Poland	c. Russia
d. France	e. Egypt	f. Iraq
g. India	h. Myanmar	i. Saudi Arabia
j. Mongolia	k. Iran	l. Turkey
m. Nigeria	n. Kenya	

3a. Cape Town	b. Berlin
c. London	d. Moscow
e. Ankara	f. New Delhi
g. Kano	h. Paris

A. Pretest (p. 18)

1.	Turkey, Asia	2.	Norway, Europe
3.	England, Europe	4.	China, Asia
5.	Italy, Europe	6.	China, Asia
7.	Japan, Asia	8.	India, Asia
9.	Australia, Australia	10.	Indonesia, Asia
11.	Denmark, Europe	12.	Philippines, Asia
13.	Nigeria, Africa	14.	Egypt, Africa
15.	Russia, Europe	16.	Egypt, Africa
17.	Hungary, Europe	18.	India, Asia
19.	South Korea, Asia	20.	Pakistan, Asia
21.	Thailand, Asia	22.	Russia, Europe
23.	France, Europe	24.	Australia, Australia
25.	Germany, Europe		

A. Test (p. 19)

1.	a, d	2.	c, d
3.	a, a	4.	b, a
5.	b, c	6.	b, d
7.	b, a	8.	d, b
9.	c, b	10.	a, d
11.	c, d	12.	b, a
13.	a, a	14.	d, a
15.	b, d		

Unit 4: Physical Features
A. Europe (p. 20–24)

1.

A. a	B. a, b	C. d
D. a	E. a, c	F. b
G. a, c	H. a, c	I. a

2.

a. b	b. c	c. c
d. d	e. a	f. b
g. a, b, c	h. a	i. b
j. c	k. a	l. a

3A. c   B. a, b, c   C. a

4.

A. a, f	B. e	C. c, d
D. b		

5 I. a   II. b   III. e
IV. c   V. d   VI. f

A. Pretest (p. 25–26)

1.	Thames	2.	Kjolen
3.	Po	4.	North European
5.	Pyrenees	6.	Aegean
7.	Seine	8.	Baltic
9.	Carpathians	10.	Black
11.	Jutland	12.	Iberian
13.	Volga	14.	Urals
15.	Dneiper	16.	Adriatic
17.	Danube	18.	Alps
19.	Hungarian	20.	Wallachian
21.	Mediterranean	22.	Caucasus
23.	Vistula	24.	Ebro

A. Test (p. 27)

1.	b	2.	a	3.	b	4.	a
5.	a	6.	d	7.	d	8.	b
9.	b	10.	c	11.	a	12.	b
13.	c	14.	a	15.	b		

B. Asia (p. 28–34)

1.

A. c	B. c	C. a, d
D. a, b	E. a	F. d
2a. b, c	b. c	c. a, c
d. a, c	e. a, b	f. b, c, d
g. d	h. b	

3.

A. a	B. c	C. c
D. a	E. b	F. a, b
G. c	H. d	

4.   a, c, f, g, h, j, l
5.   a, d, f, g, j
6.

I. e	II. a	III. b
IV. g	V. h	VI. f
VII. d	VIII. c	IX. i

7A. b   B. a   C. a

B. Pretest (p. 35)

1.	Elburz	2.	Indus
3.	Kyzylkum	4.	Irrawaddy
5.	Himalayas	6.	Karakum
7.	Huang Ho	8.	Thar
9.	Takla Makan		
10.	Western Ghats, Eastern Ghats		
11.	Ganges	12.	Caspian
13.	Gobi	14.	Aral
15.	Tigris, Euphrates	16.	Yangtze
17.	Arabian	18.	Amur
19.	Red	20.	South China

B. Test (p. 37)

1.	c	2.	b	3.	a	4.	c
5.	b	6.	d	7.	b	8.	b
9.	d	10.	b	11.	d	12.	c
13.	d	14.	a	15.	c		

C. Africa (p. 38–40)

1.

A. a, c	B. a	C. b
D. a	E. b	

2a. b   b. a   c. a, c
   d. a, c, d   e. d   f. a, c, d
   g. a, b, c

3. 1.   a, b, d   2. c 3. b, d
   4.   b
4. 1. a, c   2. a, b, c   3. a, c
   4.   c, d   5. a, c

5. Tanzania, Kenya, Zambia, Democratic Republic of the Congo, Malawi

C. Pretest (p. 41)

1.	Lake Victoria	2.	Mt. Kilimanjaro
3.	Lake Tanganyika	4.	Nile
5.	Congo	6.	Lake Chad
7.	Kalahari	8.	Mt. Kenya
9.	Atlas	10.	Drakensberg
11.	Zambezi	12.	Great Rift Valley
13.	Sahara		

C. Test (p. 42)

1.	d	2.	a	3.	a	4.	a
5.	d	6.	b	7.	a	8.	c
9.	c	10.	a	11.	c	12.	d
13.	c						

D. Australia (p. 43–44)

1., 10. Teacher check Map 15.

2.	b, d	3.	d	4.	a, b
5.	c, d	6.	b, d	7.	d
8.	b	9.	a		

D. Pretest (p. 48)

1.	Great Dividing Range	2.	Darling
3.	Western Australia	4.	Australia
5.	New Zealand	6.	Tasmania
7.	Indonesia		
8.	Gibson, Great Victoria, Great Sandy		
9.	Murray	10.	Great Barrier Reef

D. Test (p. 46)

1.	c	2.	b	3.	a	4.	c
5.	a	6.	d	7.	b	8.	b
9.	c	10.	b				

Unit 5: More About the Function of Cities

A. Cities Serve a Function (p. 47–54)

1. Cities in Europe

a. c; France; government, transportation, tourist, trade
b. b; Italy; government, transportaton, tourist
c. d; Italy; transportation, tourist, finance, trade, manufacturing
d. c, Germany; transportation, manufacturing
e. b, Poland; government, transportation, manufacturing
f. a, Hungary; government, transportation, tourist, trade, manufacturing
g. a, England; government, transportation, tourist, finance, trade

2. Cities in Asia

a. c, India; transportation, trade, manufacturing
b. d, China; government, transportation, trade, manufacturing
c. b, China; transportation, trade, manufacturing
d. d, Singapore; transportation, finance, trade, manufacturing
e. b, Japan; government, transportation, finance, trade, manufacturing

3. Cities in Africa

a. b, Kenya; government, transportation, finance, trade, manufacturing
b. b, South Africa; trade, manufacturing, mining
c. d, Mali; government, trade
d. c, Egypt; government, transportation, tourist, trade
e. c; Nigeria; transportation, trade
f. a; South Africa; government, transportation, tourist, trade

4. Cities in Australia

a. c; government, transportation, trade, mining
b. a; government, transportation, tourist, finance, trade, manufacturing

Unit 6: Using Latitude and Longitude in the Eastern Hemisphere

A. Using Latitude and Longitude (p. 55–56)

1.	Teacher check.	2.	Teacher check.
3.	a	4.	b
5.	a, d	6.	Teacher check.
7.	c	8.	a
9.	b, c	10.	15N, 120W
11.	45N, 60W	12.	30N, 0
13.	30S, 60W	14.	60N, 60E
15.	60S, 90E	16.	30N, 150E

A. Map 16 Activity (p. 57–58)

1.	a	2.	d	3.	b	4.	c
5.	a	6.	d	7.	c	8.	a
9.	c	10.	a	11.	a	12.	a
13.	b						

A. Pretest (p. 59)

1.	equator	2.	Prime Meridian
3.	equator	4.	Prime Meridian
5.	180	6.	parallel
7.	poles	8.	90
9.	Northern	10.	Southern
11.	Eastern	12.	Western
13.	west, north	14.	east, south

A. Test (p. 60)

1.	b	2.	a	3.	b	4.	a
5.	d	6.	c	7.	c	8.	c
9.	a	10.	c	11.	d	12.	b
13.	b, c	14.	a, c				

B. Determining the Time for Cities Located at Different Longitudes (p. 61–62)
1. Teacher check.   2. b
3. a   4. b   5. b
6. d   7. b   8. c
9. a   10. b   11. c
12. a   13. c   14. a

B. Map 17 Activity (p. 63–64)
1. Teacher check   2. b   3. b
4. a   5. b   6. d   7. b
8. c   9. a   10. d   11. b
12. a   13. c   14. b   15. b

C. Using Latitude and Longitude to Determine Distance Between Locations (p. 65)
1. c   2. c   3. c   4. b
5. a   6. b   7. b   8. d
9. c

Unit 7: Climate
A. Tundra (p. 66)
1. Teacher check Map 18.
2. Norway, Russia, Finland, Sweden
3. Murmansk   4. c

B. Subarctic (Taiga) (p. 66–67)
1. Teacher check Map 18.
2. Finland, Sweden, Norway, Russia
3. b   4. c

C. Humid Continental (p. 67)
1. Teacher check Map 18.
2. Norway, Poland, Sweden, Ukraine, Russia
3. c   4. c

D. West Coast Marine (p. 68)
1. Teacher check Map 18.
2. b   3. b
4. England, Norway, Sweden, Slovakia, Ireland, Denmark, New Zealand, Australia, South Africa
5. c

E. Mediterranean (p. 68–69)
1. Teacher check Map 18.
2. a   3. b
4. Spain, Morocco, Italy, Greece, Israel, Turkey, Australia, Algeria
5. c

F. Steppe or Semiarid (p. 69)
1. Teacher check Map 18.
2. b   3. T
4. China, Australia, Iraq, Iran, Syria, Angola, Mali, Pakistan, Morocco
5. F

G. Desert (p. 70)
1. Teacher check Map 18.
2. Saudi Arabia, Australia, Iran, Pakistan, Angola, Niger, China, Chad, Libya, Algeria, Sudan, Burkina Faso
3. Saudi Arabia, Libya, Egypt, Niger, Mali, Uzbekistan

H. Tropical Rain Forest (p. 70)
1. Teacher check Map 18.
2. Gabon, Democratic Republic of the Congo, Congo, Indonesia, Malaysia
3. b   4. d

I. Tropical Savanna (p. 71)
1. Teacher check Map 18.
2. Australia, Chad, India, Vietnam, Democratic Republic of the Congo, Angola, Thailand, Cambodia
3. T   4. F

J. Humid Subtropical (p. 71–72)
1. Teacher check Map 18.
2. Japan, China, Australia, South Korea
3. T   4. T

K. Highland (p. 72)
1. Teacher check Map 18.
2. Nepal, China, Switzerland
3. b   4. c   5. a

L. Identifying Climates (p. 74)
Teacher check Map 18.
1. London, west coast marine, England, Europe
2. Cape Town, mediterranean, South Africa, Africa
3. Bombay, tropical rain forest, India, Asia
4. Moscow, humid continental, Russia, Europe
5. Canberra, west coast marine, Australia, Australia
6–10. Answers will vary. Accept answers based on climates and seasons.

L. Identifying Climates (p. 75)
1. Tundra: Asia, Europe
2. Tropical Rain Forest: Africa, Asia
3. West Coast Marine: Africa, Australia, Europe
4. Mediterranean: Africa, Australia, Asia, Europe
5. Humid Continental: Asia, Europe
6. Subarctic: Asia, Europe
7. Steppe: Africa, Australia, Asia, Europe
8. Desert: Africa, Australia, Asia
9. Highland: Africa, Asia, Europe
10. Tropical Savanna: Africa, Australia, Asia
11. Humid Subtropical: Australia, Asia
12. c   13. b

L. Identifying Climates—Pretest Practice (p. 76)
1. highland
2. China
3. humid subtropical
4. Mediterranean
5. tropical rain forest
6. west coast marine
7. desert
8. tundra
9. tropical rain forest
10. Mediterranean
11. 3.3
12. tropical rain forest

L. Identifying Climates—Test (p. 77)
1. a
2. c
3. d
4. a
5. b
6. b
7. a
8. d
9. a
10. c

Unit 8: Understanding Developed and Under-developed Countries

A. Population Pyramids (p. 78–80)
Country A
1. c
2. a
3. a
4. c
5. a

Country B
1. a
2. a
3. b
4. d
5. b

Pyramid C
Pluses should be on 1, 3, and 5.

Pyramid D
Pluses should be on 7 and 9.

B. Population Density (p. 81)
1. 146
2. 79
3. 211
4. 336
5. 173
6. b
7. b

B. Population Density (p. 82–83)
Teacher check Maps 19 and 20.
1. c
2. a
3. c
4. b
5. a
6. a
7. b
8. c
9. b

C. Subsistence Agriculture vs. Manufacturing (p. 84)
1. a, a
2. b, b
3. All statements should have a plus sign.

D. Gross National Product (p. 85–86)
CHART I
1. Europe
2. Europe
3. Europe
4. Asia
5. Europe
6. Europe
7. Europe
8. Europe

CHART II
9. Africa
10. Africa
11. Africa
12. Africa
13. Africa
14. Africa
15. Africa
16. Africa
17. Africa
18. b
19. d
20. b

Unit 9: Reading Exercises to Determine the Country (p. 87–89)
1. b
2. a
3. c
4. b
5. b
6. c
7. c
8. c
9. a

Unit 10: Regions of Conflict
A. Conflict Between Countries
1. North Korea and South Korea (p. 90–91)
1–4. Teacher check Map 21.
5. c
6. c
7–8. Teacher check Map 21.

2. India and Pakistan (p. 92)
1–3. Teacher check Map 21.
4. b
5. a

3. Israel and Palestine (p. 93–94)
1–8. Teacher check Map 22.
9. c
10. b

B. Conflict Within Countries
1. The Balkan Peninsula (p. 95–97)
1–6. Teacher check Map 23.
7. a
8. c
9. d
10. Hungary, Romania
1–12. Teacher check Map 24.
13. Slovenia, Albania, Croatia, Montenegro, Bosnia and Herzegovina
14. Bulgaria, Romania
15. Greece
16. d
17. a
18. b
19. c

2. Democratic Republic of the Congo (p. 98–99)
1–14. Teacher check Map 25.

Unit 11: Strategically Important Countries
A. Location (p. 100–102)
1. a
2. d
3. c
4. d
5. a
6. a
7. c
8. c
9. a
10. b
11. c
12. d
13. d
14. b
15. c
16. d
17. a
18. b
19. c
20. d
21.
a. Africa, North Africa
b. Africa, North Africa
c. Africa, North Africa
d. Africa, North Africa
e. Asia, Middle East
f. Asia, Middle East
g. Asia, Middle East
h. Asia, Middle East
i. Asia, Middle East
j. Asia, Middle East
k. Asia, Middle East
l. Asia, Middle East
m. Asia, Central Asia
n. Asia, Central Asia
o. Asia, Central Asia
p. Asia, Central Asia
q. Asia, Central Asia

r. Asia, Caucasus Region
s. Asia, Caucasus Region
t. Asia, Caucasus Region

B.   Oil Reserves (p. 103)
Pluses should be on Algeria, Tunisia, Libya, Egypt, Iraq, Saudi Arabia, Yemen, Iran, Azerbaijan, Turkmenistan, Kazakhstan

B.   Oil Reserves (p. 104)
1. e   2. a   3. c   4. d
5. b   6. a   7. c
8. Teacher check Map 28.
9. Strait of Gibraltar, Mediterranean Sea, Aegean Sea, Dardanelles, Sea of Marmara, Bosporus, Black Sea

C.   Religion (p. 106–107)
1. Algeria, Egypt, Iran, Iraq, Saudi Arabia, Jordan, Syria, Libya, Tunisia, Azerbaijan, Kazakhstan, Tajikistan, Turkmenistan, Uzbekistan
2. Israel
3. Georgia, Armenia
4. Armenia, Georgia, Lebanon

C.   Religion (p. 108–109)
1–8. Teacher check Map 30.
9. c   10. a   11. b   12. c

Unit 12: Man and the Environment
A.   Desertification (p. 110)
1. c   2. a   3. c

B.   Salinization (p. 111–112)
1. b   2. c   3. a   4. d
5. b   6. a   7. c   8. a
9. b   10. c   11. a   12. c

C.   Flooding (p. 113)
Teacher check Maps 33a and 33b.

Unit 13: Solve These Problems
PROBLEM 1 (p. 114)
1. b   2. d
3. Sierra Leone   4. South Africa
5. South Africa   6. Sierra Leone
7. Sierra Leone   8. South Africa
9. Sierra Leone   10. South Africa

PROBLEM 1 (cont.) (p. 115)
1. 7. $71.65, $309.95
   8. $71.65, 0.20, $14.33, $85.98, $395.93
2. c   3. c   4. c   5. b

PROBLEM 2 (p. 116–117)
1. c   2. b   3. d   4. a
5. b   6. a   7. c   8. d
9. a   10. c   11. b   12. b
13. Plus signs should be on b, e, f, h, i, and k.
14. Answers will vary.

PROBLEM 3 (p. 118)
Table I
1. c   2. a   3. b   4. c
Table II
1. b   2. c   3. c   4. b

PROBLEM 3 cont. (p. 119)
Table I
1. c   2. a   3. c   4. a
5. a   6. c
Table II
1. c   2. b   3. a   4. c
5. a   6. c

PROBLEM 4 (p. 120)
1. c   2. c